EVALUATION OF ARCHAEOLOGICAL DECISION-MAKING PROCESSES AND SAMPLING STRATEGIES

European Regional Development Fund Interreg IIC
- Planarch Project

by Gill Hey and Mark Lacey

with contributions by Neil Linford, Andrew David and Nick Shepherd

OXFORD ARCHAEOLOGICAL UNIT

Printed in Oxford, England by Alden Group Limited
ISBN 0904 220 265

Preface

The introduction of PPG 16 in 1990 has resulted in a considerable increase in archaeological evaluation, as archaeology is more and more integrated within the planning system. How can effective mitigation strategies be devised and in particular how can approaches to sampling be applied to evaluation, which both pass the test of planning reasonableness in respect of cost and other constraints and yet can be relied on for accurate prediction in relation to archaeological realities on and under the ground?

A variety of approaches has been developed over the years, including desk-based survey, fieldwalking, geophysical survey, boreholing and, of course, the ubiquitous trial-trenching in its various forms. Many of these techniques go back way before PPG 16 and time has seen their refinement. There has, however, been little systematic appraisal of the suitability of these tools for the job in hand and, in spite of notable progress in some areas, in others, either through inertia or tradition, there has perhaps been a tendency for past practices to be uncritically reinforced in the present. Thus, for example, 2% trial-trenching has perhaps become an industry norm in some areas, with archaeological practitioners failing to realise that such a scheme was devised with the specific objective of finding ring ditches in Berkshire: the approach was mathematically based and carefully thought through to give a high probability of locating ring ditches 40 m in diameter within a specific landscape context. There is a clear warning to us all not to become archaeological lemmings.

Alongside the integration of archaeology in planning, recent years have seen increasing co-operation between European archaeologists with the establishment of European Association of Archaeologists and the European Archaeological Council, which brings together the various state archaeological services across Europe. It is appropriate, therefore, that approaches to archaeological evaluation are reviewed within the framework of the Interreg IIC programme for the North West Metropolitan Area (NWMA) which is very much concerned with spatial planning issues and is supported by the European Regional Development Fund. For its part, English Heritage has been pleased to support a project which is making a significant contribution to taking forward best practice in archaeological evaluation and to the further integration of archaeology within the planning process.

David Miles   -   Chief Archaeologist, English Heritage
John Williams   -   Head of Heritage Conservation, Kent County Council and Chairman of the Planarch Project

CONTENTS

List of figures   iv

List of tables   v

Summary   vii

Acknowledgements   xv

1   Introduction   1
     1.1   Background and previous work   1
     1.2   The key issues and circumstances of the project   1
     1.3   The sites selected for examination   2
     1.4   Aim and objectives of the project   5

2   Method   6
     2.1   Assessing evaluation strategies and decision-making processes   6
     2.2   Analysis of geophysical results   10
     2.3   Assessing alternative strategies   10
     2.4   Assessing Best Value   12

3   Results: assessment of evaluation techniques employed   14
     3.1   The sites   14
     3.2   Success of techniques in relation to physical characteristics of sites   15
     3.3   The success of different techniques   21
     3.4   Assessing different aspects of the archaeological remains   32

4   Results: computer simulations   34
     4.1   Comparison between the trench arrays   34
     4.2   Comparison between the different sample fractions   43
     4.3   Assessing variability   45
     4.4   Summary of results   48
     4.5   Independently evaluating simulations   49

5   Cost-effectiveness   52
     5.1   The cost of evaluation   52
     5.2   Strip, map and sample   55

6   Conclusions   58
     6.1   Evaluation methods in relation to physical circumstances   58
     6.2   Non-intrusive evaluation methods   58
     6.3   Intrusive methods of evaluation and the results of computer simulations   58
     6.4   Evaluation in relation to different periods and types of archaeological remains   59
     6.5   Implications for the decision-making process   61
     6.6   The way forward   63

7   Bibliography   64

Appendix 1   Site questionnaire   67

Appendix 2   Study of geophysical surveys, *by Neil Linford and Andrew David*   76

Appendix 3   Detailed methodology of the computer simulations, and their results   90

List of Figures

Figure 1	Location of the sites in the study area	3
Figure 2	Geophysics and machine trenching at Yarnton, Site 7	4
Figure 3	Form used to assess success of evaluation techniques	8
Figure 4	Success of techniques in relation to size of project, A All periods, B Roman period, and C Iron Age period	17
Figure 5	Success of techniques in relation to shape of project	19
Figure 6	Success of techniques in relation to geology	19
Figure 7	Success of techniques in relation to colluvium/alluvium	20
Figure 8	Success of techniques in relation to depth of overburden	20
Figure 9	Success of techniques in relation to recent land use	21
Figure 10	Success of desk-based assessment by period	22
Figure 11	Success of fieldwalking by period	24
Figure 12	Fieldwalking at Thurnham Villa, Roman pottery	25
Figure 13	Fieldwalking at Stansted, Prehistoric pottery	25
Figure 14	Success of geophysical surveys by period	26
Figure 15	Magnetometer survey at Yarnton Site 5	27
Figure 16	Excavated features at Westhawk Farm	28
Figure 17	Geophysical survey results overlain on excavated features at Westhawk Farm	29
Figure 18	Success of machine trenching by period	30
Figure 19	Thurnham Villa, actual trenching (3%)	31
Figure 20	The simulated trench arrays	34
Figure 21	Thurnham Villa with 5% standard grid array	38
Figure 22	White Horse Stone with 10% parallel trenches	39
Figure 23	Comparison of success of standard grid and parallel trenches (Arrays 1 and 4)	40
Figure 24	White Horse Stone with grid array of wide trenches	40
Figure 25	The 'Ramsgate Harbour' Array	41
Figure 26	Comparative success of different trench arrays	42
Figure 27	Improvement of success as sample size increases: grid and parallel trenching	43
Figure 28	Improvement in success rate as sample size increases for different periods	44
Figure 29	Westhawk Farm with 3% trenching	46
Figure 30	Westhawk Farm: archaeological features exposed in 3% trenches	47
Figure 31	Relative cost of evaluation techniques	53
Figure 32	Success of techniques for all periods	53
Figure 33	Increase in cost in relation to increased trenching	55
Figure 34	Success of techniques for Neolithic/Bronze Age period	60
Figure 35	Success of techniques for Iron Age period	60

Figure 36   Success of techniques for Roman period   61

Figure 37   Success of techniques for early medieval (Anglo-Saxon) period   61

Figure 38   Success of techniques for medieval period   61

Figure 39   Westhawk Farm: archaeological features superimposed over a false
                 colour image illustrating spatial analysis of the geophysical survey
                 interpretation   82

Figure 40   Yarnton Cresswell Field: archaeological features superimposed over a
                 false colour image illustrating spatial analysis of the geophysical survey
                 interpretation   84

Figure 41   Yarnton Site 5: archaeological features superimposed over a false
                 colour image illustrating spatial analysis of the geophysical survey
                 interpretation   84

Figure 42   Thurnham Roman Villa: archaeological features superimposed over
                 a false colour image illustrating spatial analysis of the geophysical
                 survey interpretation   85

Figure 43   Thanet Way: archaeological features superimposed over a false
                 colour image illustrating spatial analysis of the geophysical survey
                 interpretation   87

List of Tables

Table 1   The scoring system   9

Table 2   Physical attributes of the sites   14

Table 3   Evaluation techniques employed   15

Table 4   Periods present on projects studied   16

Table 5   Simulations undertaken   35

Table 6   Simulation results for different arrays for all archaeology
                 and by period   37

Table 7   Results of quantification calculations, showing
                 archaeology discovered   45

Table 8   The results of best- and worst-trench positions   48

Table 9   Results of moving trenches a regular distance   49

Table A1.1   Questionnaire: initial information   67

Table A1.2   Questionnaire: desk-based assessment   68

Table A1.3   Questionnaire: fieldwalking   69

Table A1.4   Questionnaire: geophysical survey   70

Table A1.5   Questionnaire: test pits and boreholes   71

Table A1.6   Questionnaire: trench evaluation   72

Table A1.7   Questionnaire: excavation   73

Table A1.8   Questionnaire: watching brief   74

Table A1.9   Questionnaire: other information   75

Table A2.1   The sites and surveys   78

Table A2.2   Results of analysis of geophysical surveys   81

Table A3.1	Quantification of the success of the simulations (random positions): All archaeology	93
Table A3.2	Simulation results (random positions): Neolithic and Bronze Age	94
Table A3.3	Simulation results (random positions): Iron Age	95
Table A3.4	Simulation results (random positions): Roman	96
Table A3.5	Simulation results (random positions): Early medieval/Anglo-Saxon	97
Table A3.6	Simulation results (random positions): Medieval	98

Summary

This pilot study, undertaken by the Oxford Archaeological Unit at the behest of Kent County Council, has examined the archaeological decision-making processes and the actual and potential sampling strategies on some major infrastructure projects carried out in south-east England in the last decade. The project was funded by English Heritage and the European Regional Development Fund, as part of its Interreg IIC programme.

The twelve projects selected for study provided a range of types and periods of archaeology in a variety of topographical circumstances with diverse land-use histories. The c 240 hectares covered by these projects had been evaluated by a suite of techniques, and very large areas had subsequently been examined and planned during excavation and watching brief. Thus it was possible to compare the predictions made at evaluation stage with the remains encountered in fieldwork over a very large area. A crucial element of the study was the computer simulation of alternative trenching strategies upon digitised site plans, including different types of array and sample sizes.

In addition to the OAU analyses, Archaeometry Branch of English Heritage's Centre for Archaeology undertook a more detailed study of the geophysical surveys undertaken on five of these sites.

All non-intrusive methods of evaluation had merits in certain circumstances, for example desk-based assessment for developing effective strategies for evaluating sites, fieldwalking for locating sites with durable artefactual remains and prehistoric sites that only survive in the ploughsoil, and geophysics for revealing remarkable detail about feature layout for those sites with magnetically-enhanced soils. These methods were all comparatively cheap, but they all had some serious failings and none were even moderately successful at evaluating the range of archaeological remains that survived on these projects. Machine trenching was the only effective means of predicting the character of the sites in this study and, even though it was more expensive than other methods, the improved quality of information and greater certainty from which to devise a mitigation strategy, made it cost effective. In practice, all the projects adopted more than one technique of evaluation and the combination of judiciously selected methods proved to be a powerful predictive tool.

Eleven of the projects within this study had been evaluated by machine trenching, at samples of between 0.8% and 5.6%, the average being 2.4%. The simulations suggested that the proportion of the sites seen in evaluation was too small to predict with confidence the full range of archaeological material actually present upon them, and this conclusion is borne out by the unexpected discoveries made on the sites when they were stripped to examine remains of other periods. The percentage of a site that needs to be seen to assess adequately the extent and survival of archaeological remains depends on the character of the site. Where linear boundaries, substantial features and clustered remains survive, and Roman sites are obvious examples, a lower sample could be adequate, though even here 3% - 5% would be required to expect a moderately good assessment. However, more scattered and ephemeral remains, and Bronze Age and early medieval settlement sites are good examples of these, could be missed entirely by sampling at this level.

Chance evidently plays a part in site detection when trenches are placed without any knowledge of features below the ground. Experiments to assess the range of variability that can arise by the systematic but random location of trenches suggest that sampling at a given fraction can reveal up to 1.5% more or 1.5% less of the archaeology on each site than the expected proportion. This clearly makes sampling at 2% a high-risk strategy.

Trenches on the projects in this study were laid out in a grid formation, or in regard to particular features seen on air photographs or in geophysical survey, with the exception of one site that had a customised design. The grid pattern with single-width trenches 30 m or 20 m long proved to be the most effective design, along with parallel trenching, although when sample proportions reached 10% there were fewer differences between the different arrays. The size of the gaps between trenches was the most important element in trench design.

This study indicates that the single most important factor in the success of evaluating archaeological sites is the date of the remains that survive upon them, and this is true regardless of the character of the geology and topography, depth of overburden and recent land use, and it is true for all techniques of evaluation. The methods we commonly use are successfully locating Roman, medieval and, to a lesser extent, Iron Age remains, reinforcing a known bias in the archaeological record, but those of Neolithic, Bronze Age and early medieval (Anglo-Saxon) date, landscape features and those on topographies where settlement was previously thought to be absent are only being revealed as a result of extensive stripping in large infrastructure and construction projects. This suggests that we are consistently missing sites of this character. The benefits of large-scale stripping were apparent within the projects that formed part of this study, and this work suggests that serious consideration should be given in the right circumstances to stripping, planning and sampling sites (strip, map and sample), with further follow-up work concentrating on critically selected areas.

The pilot study was able to examine only twelve projects which had very diverse characteristics, and hence the general trends that can be seen in the data cannot be validated statistically. Nevertheless, it raises important issues worthy of further investigation. It is hoped that this work will prompt further studies of this kind.

alternativen Grabungsstrategien auf digitisierten Plänen der Fundstellen, einschließlich verschiedener Arten von Datenfeldern und Stichprobengrößen.

Zusätzlich zu den Analysen von OAU, führte die Archäometrische Abteilung des archäologischen Zentrums von English Heritage eine detailliertere Studie der geophysischen Vermessungsgutachten durch, die für fünf dieser Ausgrabungsorte gestellt wurden.

Alle nicht eingreifenden Methoden der Auswertung hatten ihre Vorteile unter verschiedenen Umständen, z.B. Beurteilungen vom Schreibtisch aus zur Entwicklung effektiver Strategien zur Auswertung von Ausgrabungsorten, Abgehen der Fundstellen, um Stellen mit haltbaren Artefakten und prähistorische Stätten, die nur in Ackerboden überdauern, ausfindig zu machen sowie Geophysik, um erstaunliche Details über die Merkmale der Anlagen derjenigen Stätten mit magnetisch angereicherten Böden zu enthüllen. Diese Methoden waren alle relativ preiswert, beinhalteten aber einige schwerwiegende Mängel, und waren nicht einmal einigermaßen erfolgreich bei der Einschätzung der vorhandenen Reichhaltigkeit der archäologischen Überreste, die in diesen Projekten aufgefunden wurden. Maschinelles Gräben ziehen war die einzig effektive Methode, den Charakter der Ausgrabungsorte dieser Studie zu bestimmen, und obwohl diese Methode teurer war als die anderen, war sie aufgrund der qualitativ besseren Informationen und größerer Sicherheit, woraufhin man eine Forschungsstrategie ausarbeiten kann, rentabel. Alle Projekte verwendeten in der Praxis mehr als eine Auswertungstechnik und die Kombination der vorsichtig ausgewählten Methoden erwies sich bei der Voraussage als leistungsfähiges Werkzeug.

Elf der Projekte innerhalb dieser Studie waren durch maschinelles Gräben ziehen, bei Stickproben von 0,8% und 5,6% ausgewertet worden, wobei der Durchschnittswert 2,4% entsprach. Die Simulationen legten nahe, dass die Proportion der Stätten, wie in den Auswertungen gesehen, zu klein war, um mit Sicherheit die Fülle des archäologischen Materials, das tatsächlich an ihnen vorkam, mit Sicherheit zu bestimmen und dieser Schluss erhärtet sich durch die unerwarteten Entdeckungen, die an diesen Stätten gemacht wurden, als sie abgetragen wurden, um die Überreste anderer Perioden zu untersuchen. Der Prozentsatz einer Stätte, der betrachtet werden muss, um das Ausmaß und das Überdauern archäologischer Überreste zu bestimmen, hängt vom Charakter einer Fundstelle ab. Wo lineare Abgrenzungen bestehen, überdauern beträchtliche Merkmale und zusammen gedrängte Überreste; römische Stätten sind hierfür ein offensichtliches Beispiel. Eine geringere Stichprobe könnte hierfür ausreichend sein, obwohl sogar hier 3% bis 5% benötigt würden, um eine relativ gute Betrachtung erwarten zu können. Jedoch könnten bei dieser Art Stichprobenmethode vereinzelte und ephemere Überreste, gute Beispiele hierfür sind Siedlungen aus der Bronzezeit bzw. dem Mittelalter, völlig übersehen werden.

Zufall spielt offensichtlich eine Rolle bei der Entdeckung von Stätten, wenn die Gräben ohne Wissen, was sich unter der Bodenoberfläche befindet, angelegt werden. Experimente, um die Reichweite der Variabilität zu bewerten, die sich durch die systematische, aber wahllos angelegten Gräben ergeben, deuten an, dass sich bei Stichproben zu einem bestimmten Bruchteil bis zu 1,5 % mehr bzw. 1,5% weniger archäologische Funde auf den Stätten befinden können als die erwartete Proportion. Die macht das Stichprobenverfahren mit 2% zu einer risikoreichen Strategie.

Die Gräben der Projekte in dieser Studie wurden gitterförmig angelegt oder entsprechen besonderer Merkmale, die man auf Luftaufnahmen oder anhand geophysischer Gutachten erkennen konnte, außer in einem Fall, wo man ein Stätten spezifisches Gitter anlegte. Das Gittermuster aus Gräben mit ca. 1,6m Breite und 30m bzw. 20m Länge erwies sich als am effektivsten, zusammen mit Parallelgräben, obwohl sich bei Stichprobenproportionen ab 10% weniger Unterschiede zwischen den verschiedenen Feldern ergaben. Die Größe der Abstände zwischen den Gräben war das wichtigste Merkmal bei der Konstruktion der Gräben.

Diese Studie deutet an, dass der wichtigste einzelne Faktor für den Erfolg bei der Auswertung archäologischer Stätten die Zeit ist, die die Überreste in ihnen überdauern, und dies ist ungeachtet des Charakters der Geologie und Topografie, Tiefe des aufgetragenen Materials und der Nutzung des Landes in neuerer Zeit wahr, und es trifft auch für alle

Auswertungstechniken zu. Die Methoden, die wir gewöhnlich verwenden, erweisen sich als erfolgreich bei der Ortung römischer bzw. mittelalterlicher Stätten, und in einem geringeren Ausmaß auch bei Überresten aus der Eisenzeit, was ein bekanntes Vorurteil im archäologischen Register bestätigt. Die Überreste neolithischen, bronzezeitlichen und früh mittelalterlichen (angelsächsischen) Ursprungs, Landschaftsmerkmale und diejenigen, die auf Topografien bestehen, von denen man bisher annahm, dass sie unbesiedelt waren, werden jetzt nur aufgrund umfangreicher Abtragungen in großen Infrastrukturen und bei Bauprojekten aufgedeckt. Dies deutet darauf hin, dass wir ständig Fundstellen dieses Charakters übersehen. Die Vorteile groß angelegter Abtragungen wurden in den Projekten, die Teil dieser Studie bildeten, ersichtlich und diese Arbeit deutet darauf hin, dass man unter entsprechenden Umständen ein Abtragen, unterteilen in Planquadrate und Stichproben an Fundstellen zusammen mit weiteren Arbeiten, die sich auf kritisch ausgewählte Bereiche konzentrieren, ernsthaft in Erwägung ziehen sollte.

Die Pilotstudie konnte nur zwölf Projekte untersuchen, die sehr verschiedene Charakteristiken aufwiesen, und daher kann der allgemeine Trend, der aus den Daten ersichtlich ist, nicht statistisch ausgewertet werden. Nichtsdestotrotz wirft sie einige wichtige Fragen auf, die es wert sind, weiter verfolgt zu werden. Wir erhoffen uns, dass diese Arbeit weitere Studien dieser Art nach sich ziehen wird.

(Translation by Dee Furtek)

Overzicht

Dit proefonderzoek, dat op verzoek van *Kent County Council* werd uitgevoerd door de *Oxford Archaeological Unit*, bestudeerde de besluitvormingsprocedures in de archeologie alsmede de huidige en potentiële strategieën voor bemonstering. Het onderzoek concentreerde zich op een aantal belangrijke infrastructuurprojecten die in de afgelopen tien jaar in het zuidoosten van Engeland zijn uitgevoerd. Het project werd gefinancierd door *English Heritage* en het Europese Regionale Ontwikkelingsfonds, als onderdeel van het *Interreg IIC*-programma.

De twaalf projecten die voor het onderzoek werden geselecteerd, boden een serie archeologische typen en perioden in diverse topografische omstandigheden met variërend landgebruik. De projecten strekten zich uit over circa 240 hectare, die met gebruikmaking van uiteenlopende technieken waren geëvalueerd. Sindsdien waren er zeer grote gebieden onderzocht en in kaart gebracht tijdens opgraving en archeologische begeleiding. Zo was het mogelijk om de voorspellingen die in het evaluatiestadium waren gedaan te vergelijken met de restanten die waren aangetroffen tijdens veldwerk in een zeer groot gebied. Een cruciaal element van het onderzoek was de computersimulatie van alternatieve graafstrategieën op gedigitaliseerde terreinkaarten, waarbij onder meer verschillende indelingen en monstergrootten gebruikt werden.

Naast de analyses van de OAU, nam de Archeometrie-tak van het Centrum voor Archeologie van *English Heritage* de geofysische onderzoeken onder de loep die op vijf van deze lokaties waren uitgevoerd.

Alle niet-intrusieve evaluatiemethoden hadden onder bepaalde omstandigheden hun eigen voordelen, bijvoorbeeld beoordeling in de studeerkamer voor de ontwikkeling van doeltreffende strategieën voor het evalueren van lokaties, veldonderzoek voor het vinden van lokaties met duurzame restanten van artefacten en prehistorische lokaties die alleen in de bovenste grondlagen overleven, en geofysica voor het blootleggen van opmerkelijke details over de lay-out van deze lokaties met magnetisch verrijkte aarde. Al deze methoden waren in verhouding goedkoop, maar elke methode had ernstige tekortkomingen en geen enkele was zelfs matig succesvol in het evalueren van de reeks archeologische restanten die in deze projecten gevonden zouden kunnen worden. Machinaal graven was de enige doeltreffende methode voor het voorspellen van de aard van de lokaties in dit onderzoek, en hoewel dit duurder was dan andere methoden, bleek het toch een kostenverantwoorde oplossing gezien de betere kwaliteit van de informatie en de hogere mate van zekerheid aan de hand waarvan een onderzoeksstrategie bepaald kon worden. In de praktijk werd bij alle projecten meer dan een evaluatietechniek gebruikt en deze combinatie van voorzichtig geselecteerde methoden bleek een krachtig voorspellend hulpmiddel te zijn.

Elf van de projecten in dit onderzoek zijn geëvalueerd door machinaal graven, met monsters tussen 0,8% en 5,6%, waarbij het gemiddelde 2,4% bedroeg. De simulaties suggereerden dat het deel van de lokaties dat in evaluatie gezien was, te klein was om met vertrouwen te voorspellen hoeveel archeologisch materiaal er daadwerkelijk aanwezig was, en deze gevolgtrekking werd bevestigd door de onverwachte vondsten op de lokaties toen deze werden blootgelegd om restanten van andere perioden te onderzoeken. Het percentage van een lokatie dat gezien moet worden om het aantal archeologische restanten en de toestand daarvan redelijk nauwkeurig te kunnen bepalen, is afhankelijk van de omvang van het terrein. Waar lineaire grenzen, belangrijke kenmerken en gegroepeerde restanten zijn overgebleven, en Romeinse lokaties zijn hiervan een goed voorbeeld, zou een lager percentage monsters volstaan, hoewel voor een redelijk goede beoordeling ook hier zelfs 3% - 5% vereist zou zijn. Meer verspreide en efemere resten, en het bronzen tijdperk en nederzettingen uit de vroege Middeleeuwen zijn hiervan een goed voorbeeld, kunnen bij bemonstering op dit niveau zelfs geheel over het hoofd worden gezien.

Kans speelt vanzelfsprekend een grote rol bij het vinden van lokaties wanneer sleuven worden gegraven zonder enige kennis van de kenmerken onder de grond. Experimenten voor de beoordeling van de variabiliteit die kan optreden door de systematische maar willekeurige plaatsing van sleuven, suggereren dat bemonstering bij een gegeven deel op elke lokatie tot 1,5% meer of 1,5% minder van de archeologie dan verwacht kan blootleggen. Dit bestempelt bemonstering van 2% als een strategie met hoog risico.

De sleuven op de projecten in dit onderzoek werden in rasterformatie gegraven, of met in overweging neming van kenmerken die zichtbaar waren op luchtfoto's of in geofysisch onderzoek, met uitzondering van één lokatie die een speciaal ontwerp had. Het rasterpatroon met sleuven van gelijke (standaard)breedte en 30 of 20 meter lang bleek de meest doeltreffende lay-out, samen met parallelle sleuven, maar toen de bemonstering de 10% bereikte, waren er echter minder verschillen tussen de verschillende indelingen. De omvang van de vrije ruimte tussen de sleuven was het belangrijkste element in de lay-out ervan.

Dit onderzoek wijst erop, dat de allerbelangrijkste factor voor het succes van de beoordeling van archeologische lokaties de datum is van de restanten die aldaar worden aangetroffen, en dit gaat op ongeacht de aard van de geologie en topografie, diepte van deklagen en recent landgebruik, en gaat tevens op voor alle evaluatietechnieken. De algemeen gebruikte methoden vinden met succes restanten uit de Romeinse tijd, de Middeleeuwen en, in mindere mate, het ijzeren tijdperk, hetgeen een bekende vertekening in de archeologische prestaties versterkt, maar restanten uit het Neoliticum, het bronzen tijdperk en de vroege Middeleeuwen (Angelsaksisch), kenmerken van het landschap en restanten op topografische situaties waarvan voorheen werd aangenomen dat daar nooit nederzettingen zijn geweest, worden alleen blootgelegd als resultaat van uitgebreide blootlegging in grote infrastructuur- en constructieprojecten. Dit wijst erop dat we dergelijke lokaties consequent over het hoofd zien. De voordelen van het op grote schaal blootleggen waren duidelijk voelbaar bij de projecten die deel uitmaakten van dit onderzoek, en dit werk suggereert dat onder de juiste omstandigheden het blootleggen, in kaart brengen en bemonsteren van lokaties in overweging genomen dient te worden, met latere werkzaamheden waarbij men zich concentreert op kritisch geselecteerde gebieden.

Het proefonderzoek kon slechts twaalf projecten bestuderen, elk met zeer verschillende eigenschappen, en de algemene trends die de gegevens te zien geven kunnen derhalve niet statistisch gevalideerd worden. Het onderzoek heeft echter kwesties op tafel gebracht die het waard zijn om verder onderzocht te worden. Gehoopt wordt, dat dit werk zal leiden tot verdere onderzoeken van deze aard.

(Translation by Dee Furtek)

Acknowledgements

We would like to acknowledge the help of all those who contributed to this study of evaluation techniques, particularly John Williams of Kent County Council who initiated this pilot project, and David Buckley of Essex County Council. John has been very active in promoting and advancing the study and commenting on text, and others within Kent County Council have provided help and useful comments and advice; thanks go to Lis Dyson, Paul Cuming and Simon Mason. Although fewer projects from Essex were examined during the course of this work, those at Essex County Council have provided encouragement and much useful information, especially Richard Havis who talked to us about the Stansted project.

English Heritage part-funded this study and was actively involved in its progress. Thanks are due particularly to the English Heritage Inspector, Peter Kendall, and the monitor, Sarah Jennings.

This project could not have been undertaken without the interest and help of the archaeologists involved in the projects which formed part of the study. We would like to acknowledge particularly the help of the archaeologists from Rail Link Engineering, Helen Glass, Steve Haynes and Jay Carver, who spent time in detailed discussion about the CTRL projects. Mark Atkinson and Steve Preston from Essex County Council Field Archaeology Unit talked to us about the Elms Farm site and provided much data. Wessex Archaeology allowed us to use the Tesco Manston Road, Ramsgate information and Phil Andrews discussed this with us. Thanks also go to Peter Clarke and Keith Parfitt of Canterbury Archaeological Trust, Chris Bell and Jon Nowall of Framework Archaeology and Stuart Foreman and Paul Booth of the Oxford Archaeological Unit.

This project has generated a considerable amount of interest and we would like to thank others who have contributed ideas, especially those who attended the seminar in Maidstone in August 2000. In addition, comments of the draft report have improved the final product and we are grateful particularly to Clive Orton, Kent and Essex County Councils and Rail Link Engineering. Any failings and omissions that remain are our own.

Several people within OAU were instrumental in producing this report. Nick Shepherd willingly agreed to be the guinea pig for the simulation exercise. Greg Pugh estimated the costs. Jill Hind did much of the background research, data processing and production of graphs. Klara Spandl helped with questionnaires and in interviews and Peter Lorimer produced the illustrations. Carol Allen edited the report.

Permission to use illustrations was kindly given by the following organisations: English Heritage (Figs 14 and 15); Framework Archaeology (Fig. 13); Kent County Council (Figs 16-17, 25, 29, 30, 39 and 43); Rail Link Engineering (Figs 12, 18-19, 21-22, 24 and 41); and information by Essex County Council (Fig. 13).

I INTRODUCTION

I.I Background and previous work

The pressure and speed of development over the last 20 years, tied in to changes in legislation relating to archaeology and the heritage, has led to a rapid rise in archaeological evaluation of sites in advance of development. Methods of evaluation have been devised, and have evolved, in an attempt to keep pace with changing requirements, and a number have become virtually 'standard practice', for example the 2% machine-trenched sample. However, the number of studies that have taken place to assess the effectiveness of these techniques has been few.

In 1992 English Heritage commissioned a study of archaeological assessments within the planning process, and this provided a useful review of practice then current and made recommendations about strategies employed at that time (English Heritage 1995a; Darvill et al. 1995; Champion et al. 1995). Within this project Southampton University undertook a detailed assessment of decision-making and field methods using examples in Berkshire and Hampshire (Champion et al. 1995). However, it was not possible to assess the predictions made at the evaluation stage against the reality as revealed in follow-up work.

Anecdotal evidence has continued to accumulate since then, but with little hard data against which to assess its validity. In addition, a greater variety of techniques is now in use. Concerns about the appropriate use of different methodologies have been increasing over recent years, especially following major infrastructure projects where it has been possible to undertake large-scale stripping prior to construction and where watching briefs have been possible. The inadequacies of some evaluation techniques in some circumstances have become woefully apparent. Areas deemed to be 'blanks' during the evaluation process have been seen to contain archaeological remains in subsequent work, sometimes of some significance. Certain types of site appear to be difficult to locate in the evaluation process, as do certain periods of activity. Evaluation also has a tendency to focus on detection rather than interpretation.

The proposal to undertake an up-to-date assessment of the archaeological decision-making process and sampling strategies was, therefore, timely.

I.2 The key issues and circumstances of the project

The appropriateness of evaluation techniques varies depending on geology, depth of deposits and likely character of archaeological remains. Each archaeological site is different in terms of its character and density of remains, and this has an impact on its visibility which is unrelated to its significance. Hence an Iron Age occupation site is much easier to locate than a Neolithic house, a Roman villa than a Saxon settlement. The danger of evaluation techniques is that they readily detect the highly visible, and only locate more ephemeral remains by chance, reinforcing the bias already present in the archaeological record, a concern highlighted by John Williams (1997). There has also been recent discussion about sampling strategies and their statistical basis and validity (Orton 2000, 115-47), which forms part of a body of research and literature covering sampling in archaeology and quantitative method (eg Cherry et al. 1978; Shennan 1988).

The location of each archaeological site is also variable in terms of its geology and topographical position and this affects the techniques that can be applied to its discovery. For example, geophysical survey is generally very effective on chalk, but can be poor over clay geologies. In addition, different post-depositional histories and depths of overburden have an impact on how readily archaeological features can be detected; sites buried beneath colluvium at the bottom of a slope, or by alluvium on a floodplain, are very unlikely to be found by air photography, geophysical survey or fieldwalking. Approaches adopted in many rural situations may not be applicable in an urban environment or on sites with stratification (*cf* Carver 1987), where techniques such as sub-surface digital-terrain modelling of deposits from borehole data may be of greater relevance.

Value for money is also an important issue. The most effective evaluation method may be extremely expensive, time-consuming and intrusive, and could potentially compromise a decision in favour of preservation *in situ*. Do cheaper methods in some circumstances provide an acceptable level of confidence from which to make strategic decisions? In some situations, expensive evaluation could limit, in practice, the funds available for final mitigation. Where the design of a development leaves little scope for alteration, at what stage is it more cost-effective, and more revealing of the archaeological landscape, to strip, plan and sample the entire area under threat than to evaluate and conduct more selective excavation?

All these factors must be taken into account by archaeological development-control officers and others hoping to interpret the significance of evaluation results. A clearer understanding of the impact of different variables would enable better-informed judgements to be made. Sharing experiences with colleagues in continental Europe has the potential to suggest methods of working which have not formed part of the 'British' tradition.

In order to investigate these issues in relation to decision-making within the planning process, this pilot study was initiated as part of the Planarch Project, under the European Regional Development Fund Interreg IIC programme for the North West Metropolitan Area, concerning trans-national co-operation on spatial planning. The project was part-funded by English Heritage, and a Brief was supplied by Kent County Council in April 2000 (Archive). The study was undertaken between May and early October 2000, when a draft report was submitted. The published version has been amended to take account of comments on that document.

1.3   The sites selected for examination

This pilot study was undertaken in a restricted time frame with a modest budget and, thus, the number of sites that could be investigated and the depth of the analysis on them could not be exhaustive. Following discussions with the Kent and Essex County Archaeologists and the English Heritage Inspector for Kent, twelve projects were selected for inclusion in the study (Fig. 1). They were chosen to reflect a range of infrastructure projects which have been undertaken in the two counties in recent years. In addition, OAU suggested the inclusion of the Yarnton-Cassington Project, a landscape study which was partly designed to assess the success and cost-effectiveness of evaluation techniques in alluviated areas (Hey 1994, 14). Issues which are central to the concerns of this study were also raised on the Yarnton project when remains of significance were unexpectedly discovered on sites which had already been evaluated, for example an early Neolithic building exposed on Site 7 (Fig. 2).

It was agreed that resources should be targeted to computer analysis of sites where large areas had been stripped and planned, and to modelling alternative strategies upon these. This was seen as being an aspect of the study which previously had not been investigated systematically. Projects were selected, therefore, for their suitability to undertake such analysis, as well as to provide a range of geologies, topographical situations and archaeological remains; some sites

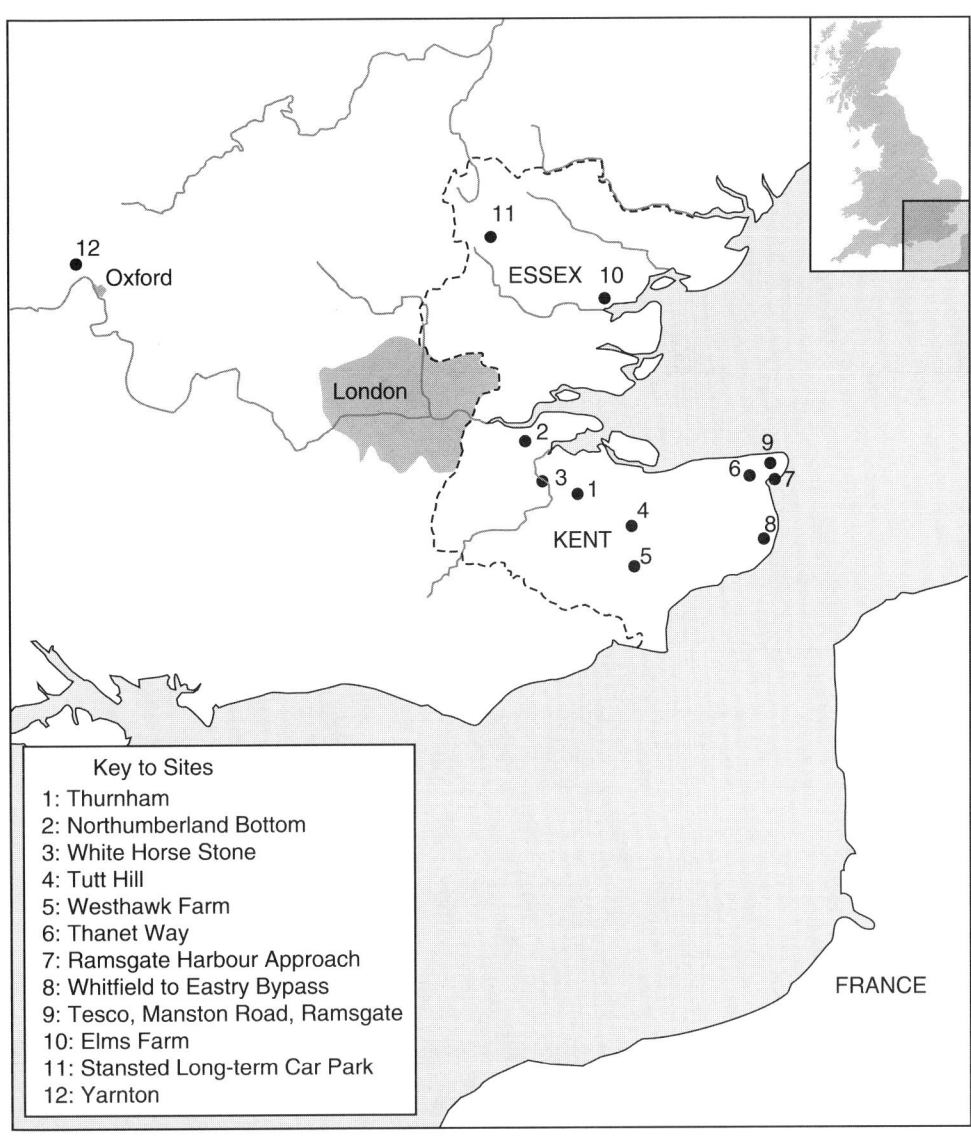

Figure 1 Location of the sites in the study area

were excluded because they had not been completed. The use of a suite of evaluation techniques in advance of excavation was also a factor in their selection. The accessibility of data in a suitable format for use digitally was an important consideration, although some time was allocated for digitising paper plans of sites which are seen as being particularly relevant to this study. Crucially, it is possible with these projects to reach conclusions based on the certain presence or absence of archaeology, as recorded on excavation and watching-brief plans.

Of the sites/projects which formed part of the study, nine were in Kent, two in Essex and one in Oxfordshire:

Thurnham, Kent: a site on the line of the Channel Tunnel Rail Link examined by the Oxford Archaeological Unit (OAU)

Northumberland Bottom to Church Road, Kent: adjacent sites on the line of the Channel Tunnel Rail Link examined by the Museum of London Archaeological Services (MoLAS)

White Horse Stone to Boarley Farm, Kent: adjacent sites on the line of the Channel Tunnel Rail Link examined by OAU and MoLAS

Westwell Leacon and Tutt Hill, Kent: adjacent sites on the line of the Channel Tunnel Rail Link examined by OAU and MoLAS

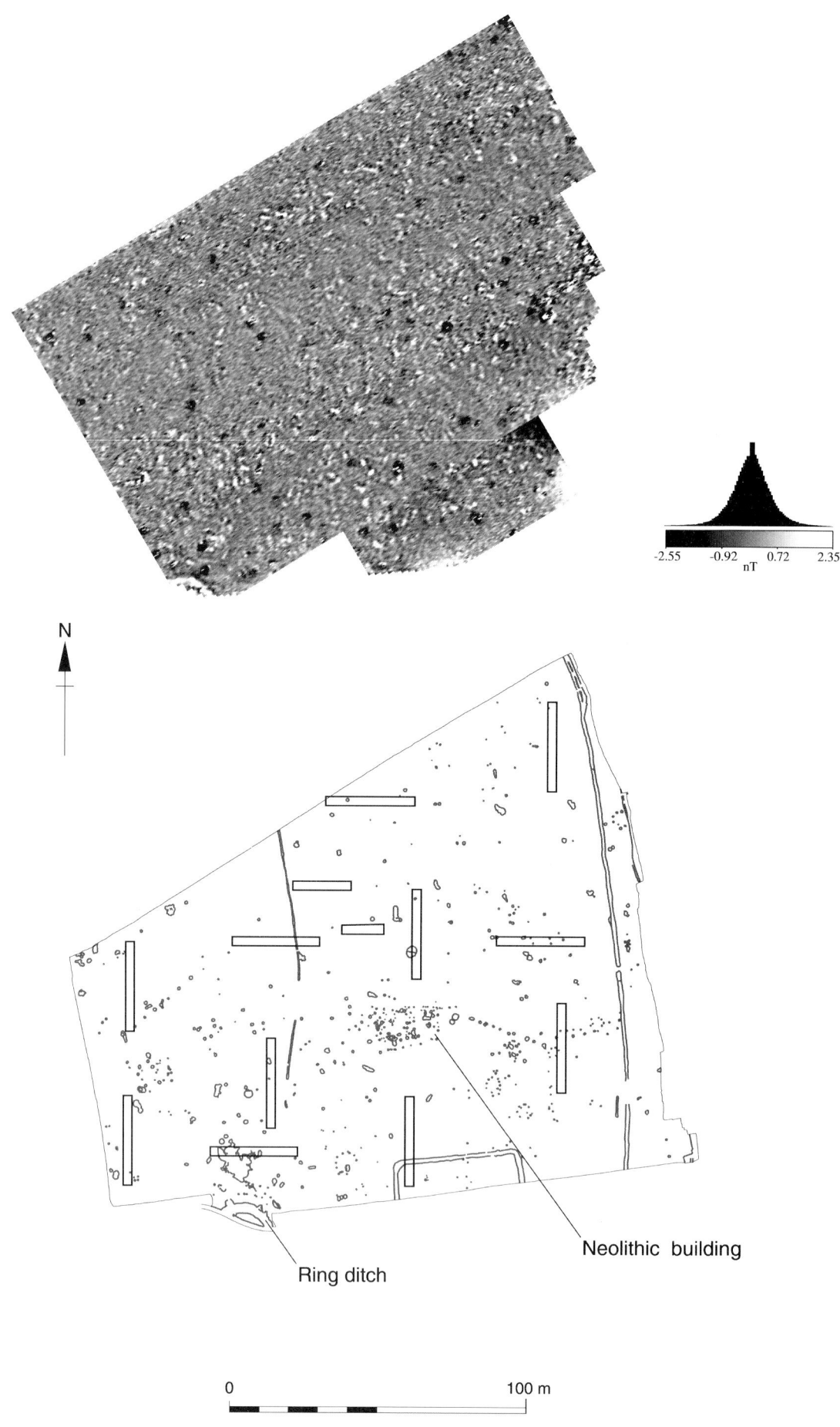

N

Neolithic building

Ring ditch

0   100 m

Figure 2 Geophysics and machine trenching at Yarnton, Site 7

Westhawk Farm, Ashford, Kent: a site evaluated by the Kent Archaeological Rescue Unit and excavated by OAU in advance of housing development

Thanet Way, Kent: A road scheme in north-east Kent examined by the Thanet Archaeological Group and Canterbury Archaeological Trust (CAT)

Ramsgate Harbour Approach Road, Kent: a road scheme in north-east Kent examined by CAT

Whitfield to Eastry Bypass, Kent: a road scheme in east Kent examined by CAT

Tesco, Manston Road, Ramsgate: a superstore development in north-east Kent examined by Wessex Archaeology

Elms Farm, Essex: a housing development in east Essex examined by Essex County Council Archaeological Group (ECC), and funded by English Heritage

Stansted, Essex: development for a long-term car park in north-west Essex, evaluated by ECC and excavated by Framework Archaeology

Yarnton, Oxfordshire: a gravel-extraction quarry in central Oxfordshire, examined by OAU and funded by English Heritage

All the projects were large in size, and of these seven related to linear schemes and five covered blocks of landscape. A variety of geologies was represented, including chalk, gravel, brickearth and clay, and some sites had subsequently been buried beneath colluvium and alluvium. The archaeological remains ranged from ephemeral and scattered Neolithic and Bronze Age sites (eg White Horse Stone, Thanet Way, Stansted and Yarnton) and dispersed Saxon settlement (eg Whitfield to Eastry Bypass, Manston Road Tesco and Yarnton) to a Roman villa at Thurnham. The character of the sites is discussed in greater detail below (Section 3.1; Table 2).

1.4   Aim and objectives of the project

In order to address the issues discussed above in Section 1.2, the Brief set out the aim and objectives of the project (Archive). The aim was to consider the effectiveness of methodologies employed in archaeological decision-making during the planning process. The objectives were:

1   To compare, for development projects that had already taken place and took place during the life of the project, the predictions of the archaeology on a given site, based on a variety of techniques, with the archaeological realities as demonstrated by further work

2   To examine whether alternative sampling strategies would have been more (or less) reliable

3   To suggest the most cost-effective approach/es to the evaluation of archaeological sites

4   To disseminate the results of the study

This is not, and was never meant to be, an assessment of the ability of individuals or organisations to evaluate or take decisions about particular sites. The projects were chosen because they were typical of infrastructure projects, throwing up a range of problems that make all these situations difficult. Projects would not have been chosen if there had been doubt about the validity of the results; it is the techniques that are under scrutiny.

2 METHOD

2.1 Assessing evaluation strategies and decision-making processes

2.1.1 Seminars

A rapid scoping exercise was undertaken followed by a presentation at a Planarch seminar in Maidstone on 2 - 4 May 2000, outlining the scope of the work and the approach to be adopted. A further seminar was held at Kent County Council Offices on 2 August for the consultees and other interested parties in Kent and Essex County Councils and English Heritage, at which the provisional conclusions were discussed.

2.1.2 Questionnaire and site database

A questionnaire was devised to assess strategies and decision-making processes for each project (Appendix 1). It was completed during the course of a series of interviews, meetings and seminars with the people who managed and/or had curatorial responsibility for the projects that were selected. These included the Kent and Essex County curators, the English Heritage Inspector and Monitor, Rail Link Engineering and site managers/directors. In summary, this stage of work collected information on:

- the character and size of the developments
- the geology, topography and depth of overburden and the type of deposits present
- the stages of decision-making and the evaluation and excavations methods employed
- the specific methodologies used in evaluation, such as sampling percentages, intervals and arrays
- the date, character, density and state of preservation of features and finds scatters located in the evaluation exercises and in subsequent excavation or watching briefs

Desk-based assessments, evaluation reports, interims and excavation reports were examined in order to supplement the data gained during interviews, and also to allow a more equable judgement of factors such as the density of remains. Examination of site plans also allowed more fair and accurate comparisons to be made between sites.

The questionnaires provided quantitative data which were entered on to an Access database.

There are many aspects of the evaluation process which are qualitative, complex, subtle and anecdotal and these cannot be analysed digitally. The interviews supplemented quantitative data by gaining the more subjective experiences of consultees. This stage of work allowed them to express their opinions on the most effective techniques employed and enabled a better understanding of the significance of the results. In addition, an appreciation was gained of the stages at which planning decisions were taken, the background to the decisions and the kinds of information that were most useful in this process.

2.1.3 Digital data

Digital mapping data were collected for all projects for which they were available, and were prepared in GIS format in AutoCAD 2000 using AutoCAD MAP. Site drawings included fieldwalking plots, interpretations of geophysical surveys, test-pit locations, evaluation trench plans, excavation and watching-brief plans. Different levels of data for individual sites were prepared on separate overlays so that results could be compared. This proved to be the most time-consuming element of the project. Aside from the time actually needed to acquire the relevant information, each project had different levels of data, often produced in different software. Standardising plans entailed some fairly substantial redrawing and data attachment for data querying. In addition, plans for some parts of most projects only existed on paper and these had to be digitised from scratch. In many cases it was necessary to create a composite plan comprising the totality of the excavated archaeology (including watching-brief results), which was often provided as a number of separate drawings representing different areas or different phases of investigation which were not easy always to correlate. Phasing information was prepared as separate layers on the site plan.

It rapidly became apparent that it was important to define rigorously the extent of the site or 'development area'. Some schemes were very extensive, especially the linear schemes such as CTRL where archaeological investigation was effectively continuous in some form or another for approximately 70 km. Individual techniques may have been attempted only on small parts of what was finally stripped and examined, or may have extended well beyond their boundaries. In order to be precise about the areas which fell within the study, to compare the different techniques on an equal basis and, most importantly, to be confident about the archaeology present in the areas evaluated, an arbitrary decision was made about the 'development areas'. These cover the formally excavated sites and the zones immediately around them. Thus there is a measure of certainty about the archaeology in the study areas, and not all evaluations undertaken on all projects were considered.

2.1.4 *Querying the data*

Once the plans were available in GIS, it was possible to compare the results of different stages of work by overlaying and interrogating the various maps. In particular, using excavation plans as a background, the results of different techniques were overlain in turn to assess their effectiveness. For example, geophysical plots were draped over excavation plans and anomalies matched with archaeological features. A series of questions was posed of each method employed on each project and the results were entered on to a form (Fig. 3). The results of the questionnaires and written reports were also taken into account during this exercise.

The effectiveness of each evaluation technique was assessed by addressing a series of questions about the results, questions which underpin most briefs and specifications for archaeological evaluations. They derive from the Secretary of State's criteria for assessing the significance of archaeological remains and are fundamental to deciding the impact of development upon archaeological sites:

1   Presence of archaeological remains
2   Location of archaeological remains
3   Density/complexity of archaeological remains
4   Character of archaeological remains
5   Layout of buried archaeological remains
6   Condition of archaeological remains
7   Quality of artefacts and ecofacts within archaeological deposits

These questions, which judged more subtle issues that simple presence/absence, were asked of the results on each site in general, and also for each period of activity present. In addition, for the sites in general the following questions were also posed:

8   Did the technique indicate the date of all the buried
     archaeology?

Figure 3 Form used to assess success of evaluation techniques

Technique	Question	All Archaeology	Neo/BA	Iron Age	Roman	Saxon	Medieval	Comments
1	Does the technique indicate the presence of sites beneath?							
2	Does the technique accurately locate the areas of activity?							
3	Does the technique reflect the intensity of buried remains?							
4	Does the technique accurately indicate the type and range of activities on site?							
5	Does the technique indicate the site layout?							
6	Does the technique reveal the conditions of the buried archaeology?							
7	Does the technique reveal the condition of the buried artefacts and ecofacts?							
	Total							
8	Does the technique indicate the quality of all the buried archaeology?							
9	Did the techniques suggest remains that were not present?							
10	Was it possible to identify accurately the features exposed by the technique? (Trenching only)							
	Total							

Scoring

0 = Poor
1 = Poor to moderate
2 = Moderate to good
3 = Good

8

9   Did the technique suggest remains that were not present?

10   Were there difficulties in identifying features exposed by the technique?

Archaeological remains were divided into five main period groups:

- *Neolithic and Bronze Age*: where funerary monuments can be expected to be the major visible component and settlement archaeology is usually ephemeral and very hard to detect
- *Iron Age*: with more dense settlement remains, but usually comprising fairly small features which can be scattered. Burials of this period are hard to locate
- *Roman*: settlement, burial and ritual sites tend to be highly visible and have abundant material remains
- *Early medieval/Anglo-Saxon*: with scattered settlement and burial evidence
- *Medieval*: where settlement is unusual in modern rural environments, and the character of these remains is varied, but evidence of land use is common (fields, boundaries, tracks etc).

Where sites spanned the late Bronze Age to early Iron Age periods, and the archaeological remains for these periods were similar, they have been classified as Iron Age.

The success of the different methods cannot be quantified easily; a judgement has to be made on the basis of the information available. Decisions of this kind are precisely those which curators deal with on a daily basis. It was decided to score success on a four-point scale (Table 1). The lowest score was set at 0 so that techniques could not accrue points by simply taking place; the score of 3 denoted good and not the best that could possibly be achieved. The decision to use a narrow range of options was deliberate. It was intended to keep the process simple and straightforward and not to assume a higher degree of accuracy than was possible given the nature of this exercise. It also limited the variability that was possible between the three individuals undertaking the analysis. In retrospect, a five- or six-point band would have provided larger numbers for statistical analysis; on the other hand there would have been less confidence in the results of such a data set, because of the greater potential to introduce inconsistencies.

Table 1 The Scoring System

Score	Result	Probable consequence
0	Poor	There would be little chance of identifying archaeological remains
1	Poor to moderate	It is unlikely, though not impossible, that the significance of the archaeological remains would be appreciated
2	Moderate to good	It is probable that the significance of the archaeological remains would be appreciated
3	Good	It is highly likely that the significance of the archaeological remains would be appreciated

Completing the forms was a time-consuming exercise, as each variable required a reasonable amount of thought, although the process speeded up as the assessor became more experienced. The scores were entered on to the database.

2.1.5   *Comparing results of evaluation techniques employed*

Using database queries, comparisons were made between the results of the techniques employed and the different kinds of remains found in excavation, in relation to different site conditions, such as geology and depth of overburden.

Scores were totalled for the success of different techniques in different circumstances. In order to allow a comparison between the methods employed, the totals were divided by the maximum possible total and multiplied by 100. Effectively they become percentages (but should not be considered as such for these are not really numerical data). In this way a poor to moderate result would achieve 33 points and a moderate to good result 67. Theoretically it is possible to achieve 100 out of 100, not by revealing all information about a site in an evaluation, but by providing good information that enables an accurate prediction of the archaeological remains present. In practice, of course, no method achieved this, although some methods did score highly for some periods.

The main difficulty posed by the results is the small number of sites (12) on which the analysis took place. This means that the statistical population is small, and eccentric results can easily skew results. Although this must be balanced against the very large area that these projects covered (240.47 ha), additional problems were posed by the fact that not all techniques were undertaken on all projects, nor were all periods of archaeological remains present in all cases. Two techniques, metal detecting and test pitting, were not used in the comparisons because they were only employed on two sites and four sites respectively (although this was not the only reason they were excluded, see below). Otherwise, in general terms, the maximum scores that could be achieved varied between 21 and 36, but for individual periods (particularly for Saxon remains which were found on only five sites) the total maximum scores are lower and should be treated with great caution. These instances are noted in the text. Finally, it must be stressed that the results are conclusions based on these projects alone.

Database queries enabled the relative success of the different techniques employed to be assessed and they were examined in relation to:

• Size and shape of the development area
• Geology
• Presence of colluvium/alluvium
• Depth of overburden and recent land use
• Different periods and types of site

Although data was gathered on the season in which evaluations took place and the prevailing ground conditions, these were too variable among the small number of projects to suggest meaningful trends.

2.2 Analysis of geophysical results

The Archaeometry Branch of the Centre for Archaeology of English Heritage kindly agreed to provide advice and undertake a comparative analysis of some of the geophysical surveys undertaken in the process of these evaluations. Owing to the limitations of the data, and the time available, this study was confined to five of the projects, and is presented as a separate study in Appendix 2.

2.3 Assessing alternative strategies

A crucial element of this project was the simulation of alternative strategies, principally trenching methods, upon the sites in this study. A variety of trench densities, sizes and arrays were modelled on separate layers in AutoCAD 2000 to overlay upon the prepared excavation and watching brief plans described above. A detailed methodology for the creation of these layers and how they were applied is described in Appendix 3.

In order to allow the computer modelling of evaluation techniques, a digitally-based site plan of the archaeological features present needed to be available in a form which allowed the differentiation of the different archaeological phases present. Furthermore, to enable quantification of the archaeological remains uncovered by the various computer simulations, the digital plan needed to be produced and 'cleaned' to a high standard. Ideally the drawing should have been generated from the outset with the objective of creating a topologically sound drawing capable of undergoing GIS analysis.

Unfortunately, it proved impossible, in the time available, to prepare all the data in such a form that every project could be subjected to the detailed quantification that was intended. It was possible to undertake some simulations on eleven of the sites, but Elms Farm, Essex presented particular problems. The Elms Farm site plan, although provided in a digital format, was not suitable for such analysis due to the extremely dense archaeology and its complex nature. The presence and depth of stratigraphy on the site meant that the resulting site plan contained numerous features overlaying each other which were very difficult to differentiate. It was decided that it was impractical to attempt any computer simulation analysis on this site, therefore, as the amount of time that would need to be spent to prepare fully the digital site plan would be beyond the scope of the project.

In addition to using overlays to observe the archaeological remains that would have been revealed in simulated evaluation trenches, it was possible to quantify the area of archaeology 'discovered' in the trenches and compare this to the total area of archaeology exposed on site plans for seven of the sites. This was undertaken for two types of array and a range of percentages (30 individual positions). However, although this was useful for assessing the variability of results which arise from the random positioning of trenches (see below), it was not very helpful for assessing the success of techniques. Judging the success of an evaluation technique solely on the area of archaeology it uncovered is grossly simplistic, as it does not consider the importance of the remains. For example, evaluation trenches may detect large lengths of a single medieval ditch, resulting in a high percentage of archaeology discovered. In contrast, the discovery of a Neolithic posthole structure and a short length of medieval ditch in evaluation would suggest that the first trenching regime was the more successful, although the second trench would be far more useful and significant in terms of the information it yielded.

For this reason, the success of simulated evaluation trench positions on the eleven sites analysed was judged in the same manner as the evaluation techniques that had actually taken place, where the questions were applicable, first considering all the archaeology as a whole, and then considering each of the five periods as before:

- Does the technique indicate the presence of sites beneath?
- Does the technique accurately locate the areas of activity?
- Does the technique reflect the intensity of buried remains?
- Does the technique accurately indicate the type and range of activities on the site?

In addition, when considering the archaeology as a whole, the following question was also posed:

- Does the technique reflect the date of all the buried archaeology?

Although the computer techniques used allow very complicated simulations and calculations to be carried out relatively rapidly, querying the success of each individual simulation required careful consideration and, for each site and each period present, a significant time input. The number of possible trenching arrays was great, and even when assessing only a limited range of sample fractions the number of simulations required rapidly multiplied to an unmanageable level. After considering over 25 types of trenching strategy, eight different trench arrays were selected for the analysis at a range of sample fractions. These are discussed below. They include the methods most commonly used in England.

Trenches were placed randomly on the site plans, taking into account the general orientation and shape of the site but without reference to the details of the excavated features (see Appendix 3). However, it was not possible to 'customise' each position by considering the impact of impediments such as overhead power cables and field boundaries that may have transected the sites, or taking into account pre-existing knowledge of the archaeology, for example from air photographs.

It is widely recognised that the chance positioning of trenches has a significant impact on the success of this evaluation technique, and the results of the simulations rapidly confirmed this. Therefore, a series of experiments was set up to assess the variability that is present within particular arrays as a result of chance. This included the quantifications already mentioned, but also:

| 1 | placing trenches deliberately to achieve the best and worst result and |
| 2 | monitoring the effect of moving one particular array a set distance of 10 m for 12 different positions. |

This is discussed in greater detail below.

One potential problem for the simulation exercise, is that the analyst becomes fairly well acquainted with the site and can see the final site plan. This, of course, is not the situation that confronts archaeologists and curators in real life; they have a very partial view of the buried remains. For six of the projects in this study, a Senior Project Manager who had not been involved in any of the sites concerned, was presented with the computer simulations at 2%, 3%, 5% and 10% in turn, showing only the archaeology within the trenches (eg as in Fig. 30). He was asked to interpret the character of archaeology from these plans and answered the following questions:

- Do there appear to be archaeological sites?
- What is the density of the archaeology (light, moderate or dense)?
- What is the character of the archaeology/range of activities (settlement, burial, ceremonial/religious, industrial, agricultural, uncertain, other)?
- Where is the most intense area/s of archaeology?
- What is the significance of the archaeology (high, moderate, low, none)?

in addition to making notes and discussing his conclusions. This independently tested the judgement of the other team members who were acquainted with the circumstances of the projects, especially the final site plans.

2.4   Assessing Best Value

An assessment of Best Value followed analysis of the results of questionnaires and interviews and the modelling of alternative strategies. This balanced the effectiveness of techniques at predicting presence of archaeology of different periods against the cost of undertaking this work, in conjunction with the difficulty of execution and the scale of disruption.

In order to assess cost-effectiveness, it was essential to know the cost of the work, at least in terms of human and machine resources. To overcome a potentially sensitive and contentious issue, and one which could introduce many variables associated with the several ways in which different organisations cost and resource projects, it was decided that the OAU tender officer should estimate the cost of evaluations and excavations on all, OAU and non-OAU, projects *de novo*, without knowing the names of the projects involved. This provided an equable basis from which to compare the different methods.

The following costs were assessed (estimates for evaluation included plant hire and report costs):

- The evaluation techniques that were undertaken on the sites
- The subsequent cost of excavation and watching briefs
- The cost of undertaking a range of evaluation sizes on the sites
- The cost of stripping, planning and sampling (at a rudimentary level), in place of evaluating in advance
- The cost of additional funds that would have had to be found after strip-map-and-sample excavation in cases where it became clear that more work needed to be undertaken (as assessed by examining the site plans).

Originally all the estimated costs of work that had actually been undertaken on these sites (evaluation and formal excavations) included plant hire, whereas those for strip-map-and-sample did not. It is normal for the cost of soil stripping in advance of excavation to be included within the excavation cost, although this is not universal, especially for large sites which can often be stripped by the developer, or their agent, as part of the overall site clearance. Stripping in advance of mapping and sampling tends to be undertaken on a different basis, as the area examined coincides with the area that would be stripped during the course of development; the costs are seldom borne by the archaeological budget. The value of the strategy relies on stripping extensive areas, often to a less-exacting standard than for formal excavation, in order to investigate the broad dynamics of settlement and other foci in the archaeological landscape (see below, Section 5.2). However, machine costs can form a significant proportion of an excavation budget and to include such costs for excavations and ignore them for strip-map-and-sample would result in unfavourable comparisons. As a result, the costs of plant were excluded from the estimates of undertaking formal excavation.

3 RESULTS: ASSESSMENT OF EVALUATION TECHNIQUES EMPLOYED

3.1 The sites

3.1.1 Physical attributes of the sites

The twelve sites selected for study covered 240.47 ha in total. The projects varied considerably in size (from 1 ha to 120 ha), and in their situation and the type of development to which they were subject (Table 2).

Seven of the projects were part of linear schemes, either railway or road construction, and five covered wider areas, either in advance of building construction projects or mineral extraction.

All projects were located in rural or semi-rural environments, and of these eleven had been subjected to ploughing to some extent; only one was entirely pasture (Elms Farm). Their siting ranged from the spurs of dry valleys to river floodplains and the underlying geology included chalk, sand, clay, brickearth and gravel (Table 2). Six of the projects had some colluvial or alluvial deposition above the archaeological horizon, and thus the depth of overburden varied from 0.15 m to 4.5 m. The average depth of soils covering the archaeology on these projects was, however, much less varied (from 0.3 m to 1 m).

Table 2 Physical attributes of the sites

Site	Development area size (ha)	Type of development and shape	Recent land use	Topography	Geology (main type)	Sub-soils	Depth of overburden	Average depth of overburden
1 Thurnham	4.4	Railway linear	Arable	Knoll at foot of downs	Clay		0.2-0.6m	0.35m
2 Northumberland Bottom	30	Railway linear	Arable	Slopes of dry valleys	Chalk	Colluvium-partial	0.15-1.2m	0.4m
3 White Horse Stone	12.4	Railway linear	Arable	Dry valleys and spurs	Chalk	Colluvium	0.2-4.5m	1m
4 Tutt Hill	8.5	Railway linear	Arable and pasture	Side of low hill	Sand	Colluvium-partial	0.43-1.05m	0.55m
5 Westhawk Farm	30	Housing area	Arable	Gently sloping	Clay		0.26-0.43m	0.4
6 Thanet Way	10	Road linear	Arable	Edge of ridge	Chalk	Colluvium-partial	0.25-0.6m	0.5m
7 Ramsgate Harbour Approach	4	Road linear	Arable	Dry valley	Brickearth	Colluvium	0.3-3m	0.4m
8 Whitfield to Eastry Bypass	1	Road linear	Arable and pasture	Low ridge	Chalk		0.25-0.3m	0.3m
9 Tesco, Manston Road, Ramsgate	1.07	Supermarket area	Arable (latterly a car park)	Edge of downland	Brickearth		0.15-0.8m	0.5m
10 Elms Farm	11.3	Housing area	Pasture	Floodplain	Gravel	Alluvium	0.2-0.4m	0.3m
11 Stansted Long-term Car Park	7.8	Car park area	Arable	Gently sloping plateau	Clay		0.19-0.62m	0.35m
12 Yarnton	120	Mineral extraction area	Arable	River terraces and floodplain	Gravel	Alluvium-partial	0.25-1.8m	0.45m
	Total= 240.47ha						0.15-4.5m range of depth	Total av= 0.46m

3.1.2 The evaluation techniques employed

A variety of evaluation techniques were employed on the twelve projects studied, as shown in Table 3. Only desk-based assessment was undertaken on all sites, but eleven sites were evaluated by machine trenching and these sampled a varied percentage of the development areas. Fieldwalking and geophysics were each

14

undertaken on seven projects, but only a small number of sites had seen any assessment by metal detecting, test pits or boreholes.

The number of machine trenches excavated at Westhawk Farm and Elms Farm was small, representing less than 1% of the development area in each case, as they were dug to supplement geophysical survey. In addition, trenches on both sites were specifically positioned to examine apparent gaps in site layout as revealed in survey. For this reason, it is unsurprising that they were relatively unsuccessful in terms of revealing the character of the site as a whole. The machine-trenching results from these two projects have been excluded, therefore, from the overall comparison of evaluation methods and the assessment of their relative success.

Table 3 Evaluation techniques employed

Site	Desk-based assessment	Fieldwalking	Metal detecting	Geophysics	Test pits/ boreholes	Evaluation trenches	Trench%	Excavation	Area excavated	Watching brief
1 Thurnham	✓	✓		✓		✓	3%	✓	4.4ha	E
2 Northumberland Bottom	✓	✓		P		✓	1.6%	✓	10.4	✓
3 White Horse Stone	✓	✓			✓	✓	2.1%	✓	12.4	✓
4 Tutt Hill	✓	✓			✓	✓	2.4%	✓	1.4	✓
5 Westhawk Farm	✓		✓	✓		P	0.6%	✓	6	
6 Thanet Way	✓			✓		P	0.4%	✓	10	E
7 Ramsgate Harbour Approach	✓		✓		✓	✓	5.6%	✓	1.05	✓
8 Whitfield to Eastry Bypass	✓	P				✓	3.2%	✓	0.56	✓
9 Tesco, Manston Rd, Ramsgate	✓					✓	4.9%	✓	1.07	
10 Elms Farm	✓			✓		P	0.8%	✓	5	
11 Stansted Long-term Car Park	✓	✓		P				✓	7.8	E
12 Yarnton	✓	✓		✓	✓	✓	1.6%	✓	15.5	✓I
	12 (100%)	7 (58%)	2 (17%)	7 (58%)	4 (33%)	11 (92%) 9 (75%)A	2.4% on average	12 (100%)		6 (50%)

P   Partial. Where technique was very limited in extent/scope
E   Development area (as defined in this study) totally excavated and, therefore, no watching brief
I   Incomplete. Where watching brief did not apply to all parts of the development
A   Adjusted total. Westhawk farm & Elms Farm excluded from trenching results (see Section 3.1.2)

3.1.3   The periods of activity present

Table 4 shows the archaeological periods present on the projects that have been studied. All sites had Neolithic or Bronze Age remains to some extent (although in some cases these were represented only by a few pits), and Iron Age settlement was also common. Only five sites had any evidence of early medieval (Anglo-Saxon) activity and few had substantial medieval remains.

3.2   Success of techniques in relation to physical characteristics of sites

In general, the number of projects was so small, and their physical attributes so varied (Table 2) that only general observations can be made about the success of techniques in different circumstances.

Table 4 Periods present on projects studied

Site	Neolithic/Bronze Age	Iron Age	Roman	Early Medieval (Anglo-Saxon)	Medieval
1 Thurnham	✓(s)	✓	✓		
2 Northumberland Bottom	✓	✓	✓		✓
3 White Horse Stone	✓	✓	✓(s)		✓(s)
4 Tutt Hill	✓	✓			
5 Westhawk Farm	✓(s)		✓		✓(s)
6 Thanet Way	✓	✓(s)	✓	✓	✓
7 Ramsgate Harbour Approach	✓	✓		✓(s)	
8 Whitfield to Eastry Bypass	✓(s)	✓		✓	
9 Tesco, Manston Rd, Ramsgate	✓			✓	✓(s)
10 Elms Farm	✓(s)	✓	✓		
11 Stansted Long-term Car Park	✓	✓	✓		✓
12 Yarnton	✓	✓	✓	✓	✓(s)
No of projects	12	10	8	5	7

(s) Small component of these sites

3.2.1 Size of development

The sizes of the projects were divided into three groups representing:

- small projects, smaller than 5 ha
- moderate projects of between 5 ha and 20 ha
- large projects, greater than 20 ha in size

On the whole, the impact of the size of a project on the success of evaluation techniques was limited (Fig. 4A). Desk-based assessments and fieldwalking were both marginally more effective on larger schemes, probably reflecting the greater scale required to assess the results which these methods produce; even so, they only achieved poor to moderate results. For geophysics the smaller sites seemed to produce the most effective results, but this is not particularly meaningful as it does not reflect the area over which the technique was used. Northumberland Bottom, for example, one of the largest projects, had one of the smallest geophysical surveys within the development area (1.1 ha). However, scale does not seem to be a critical issue for this method. Only machine trenching produced a marked difference in the results, with the larger projects yielding good results, in contrast to only moderate performances on smaller areas.

Results by period were much more variable and the small numbers of sites for some periods means that firm conclusions cannot be reached. However, it is noticeable that the size of the project had least impact on the success of finding Roman remains and most on Iron Age sites (Figs 4B and 4C), and to a lesser extent those of Neolithic and Bronze Age date.

3.2.2 Shape of development

Seven of the projects investigated were part of linear schemes, and five covered wider areas which were to be developed for various construction schemes, car parks or as quarries. Does the shape of a development have an impact on evaluating archaeological remains?

Evaluations undertaken on projects over broader areas recorded consistently higher results than those on linear schemes, but the differences were slight, especially for desk-based assessment and geophysical survey, where they were insignificant (Fig. 5).

There were greater fluctuations within the individual periods, depending on the

16

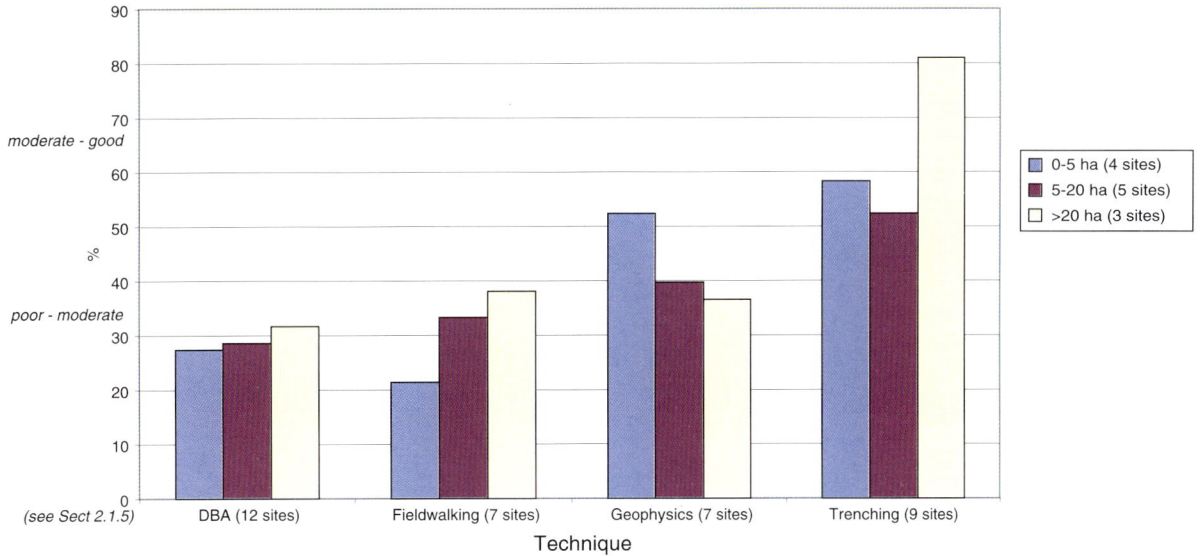

A All periods

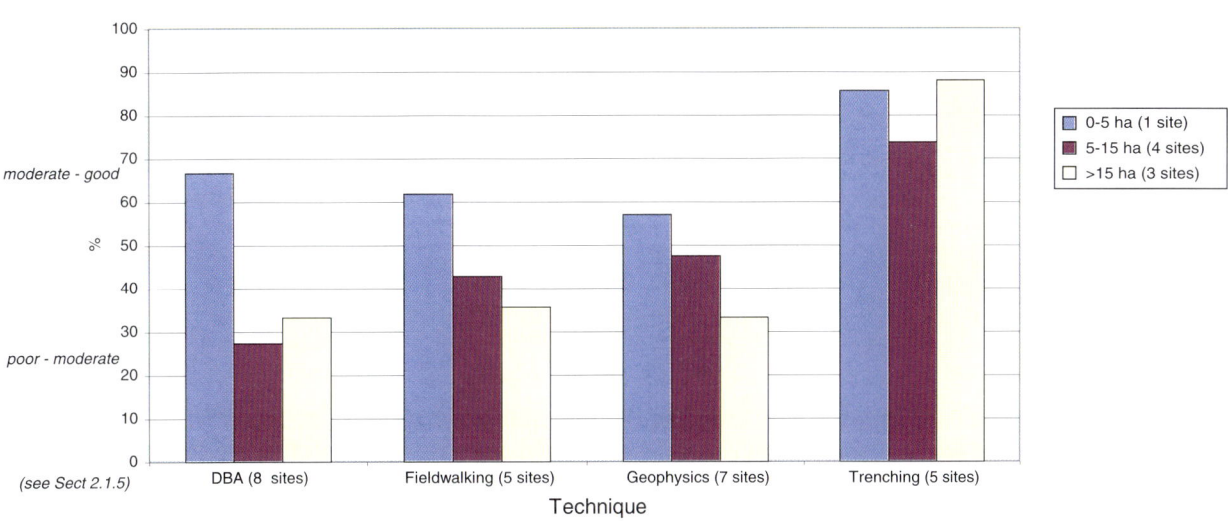

B Roman period

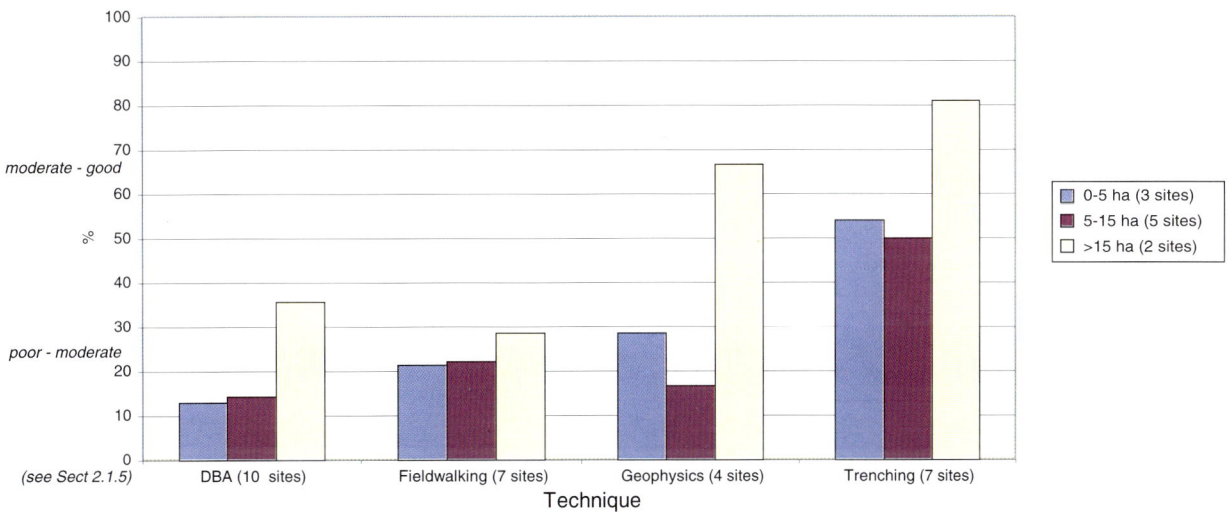

C Iron Age period

*Figure 4 Success of techniques in relation to size of project,
A All periods, B Roman period, and C Iron Age period*

characteristics of the project. Only trenching proved to be consistently more successful over blocks of landscape than on linear schemes. This is presumably the result of the comparatively long boundary between the area sampled in the evaluation and the unknown beyond.

3.2.3 Geology

There has been a good deal of discussion about the impact of geology on the effectiveness of evaluation techniques, in particular in relation to geophysical survey. In general, however, the number of sites on each of the five geologies present (Table 2) is too few to draw any meaningful conclusions about their relative attributes; individual site characteristics too easily bias the results. For example, the comparative success of fieldwalking over clay geologies is due to the fact that the only two projects on this ground for which this technique was undertaken (Thurnham Villa and Stansted) produced very good results, one of which was a Roman villa (Fig. 6).

The results indicate that for the twelve projects studied, the period of the remains had greater influence on the success of geophysical survey than the type of geology present. The very effective surveys at Westhawk Farm and Thurnham villa were undertaken on clay geologies which generally are not thought to be conducive to effective survey of this kind, but the features were mostly Roman in date and very responsive.

Once again a breakdown by period shows that differences in geology have least effect on remains of the Roman period in terms of their ease of detection. Among the Iron Age period remains within this study, sites upon gravel were evaluated most effectively.

3.2.4 Alluvium and colluvium

The presence of alluvium and colluvium on these sites (see Table 2) had relatively little impact on the effectiveness of the techniques. Only one site, Elms Farm, was completely covered by alluvium, and this was not deep. Two sites were largely covered by colluvium, White Horse Stone and Ramsgate Harbour Approach Road, and certain techniques were not conducted on them for this reason (eg geophysical survey at White Horse Stone and fieldwalking and geophysics at Ramsgate). Thus the drawbacks of these techniques in this environment are not revealed fully by this study.

Colluvial deposits provided the most difficult conditions for evaluation, but differences were slight (Fig. 7). As before, results were most consistent for the Roman period and most variable for others, but some other interesting points emerge. For the Neolithic and Bronze Age periods, partially alluviated and colluviated sites still produced magnetic responses for funerary monuments, but settlement features could not be detected by geophysics in any situation (eg Fig. 2).

3.2.5 Depth of overburden

As the extent and depth of overlying deposits was so variable, the average overburden may be a more useful way of looking at the data (Table 2).

In general terms, sites with an average overburden of more that 0.5 m were less easy to evaluate (Fig. 8). However, within most project areas there were varied topsoil depths and, in order to understand more fully the relationship between the depth of overburden and evaluation success, more time would need to be spent looking at the specific depth of soil over particular features discovered. For example, geophysics was reasonably successful at Thanet Way, the only site with an average topsoil depth of over 0.5 m on which it was attempted, but the more deeply buried parts of this project were less responsive than those with only 0.25 - 0.30 m-deep soils.

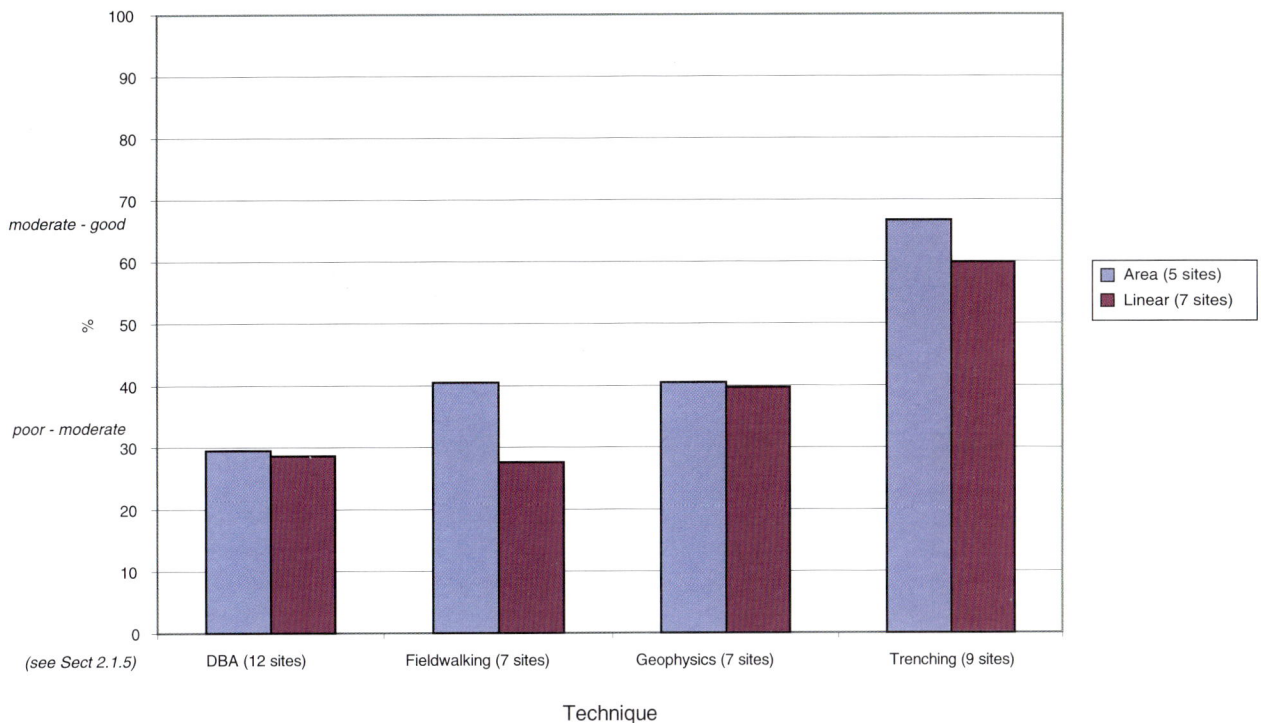

Figure 5 Success of techniques in relation to shape of project

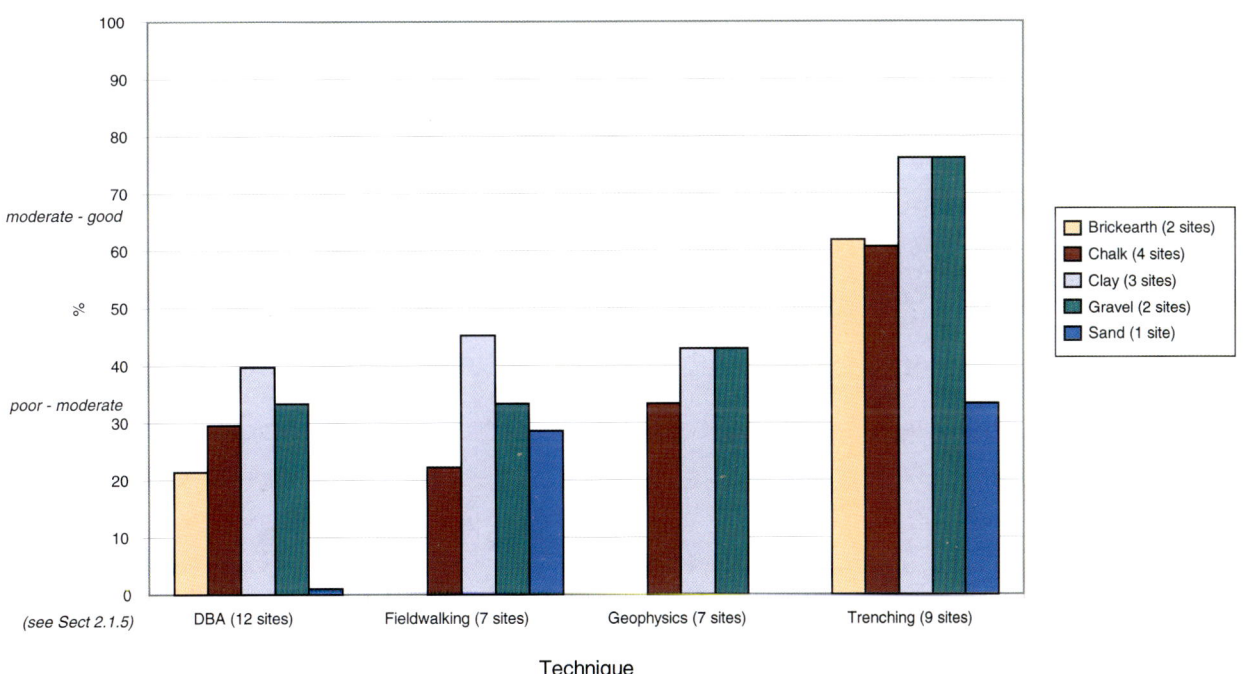

Figure 6 Success of techniques in relation to geology

On the whole, problems of overburden were recognised and fieldwalking and geophysics were much more commonly used on the shallower sites. On others, for example Yarnton, unusual circumstances (the extensive activities of Roman farmers) led to the recovery of prehistoric finds in fieldwalking on the floodplain (Hey 1998).

The success of evaluating sites with different depths of overburden varied a good deal by period, although less for the Roman period than any other. Iron Age

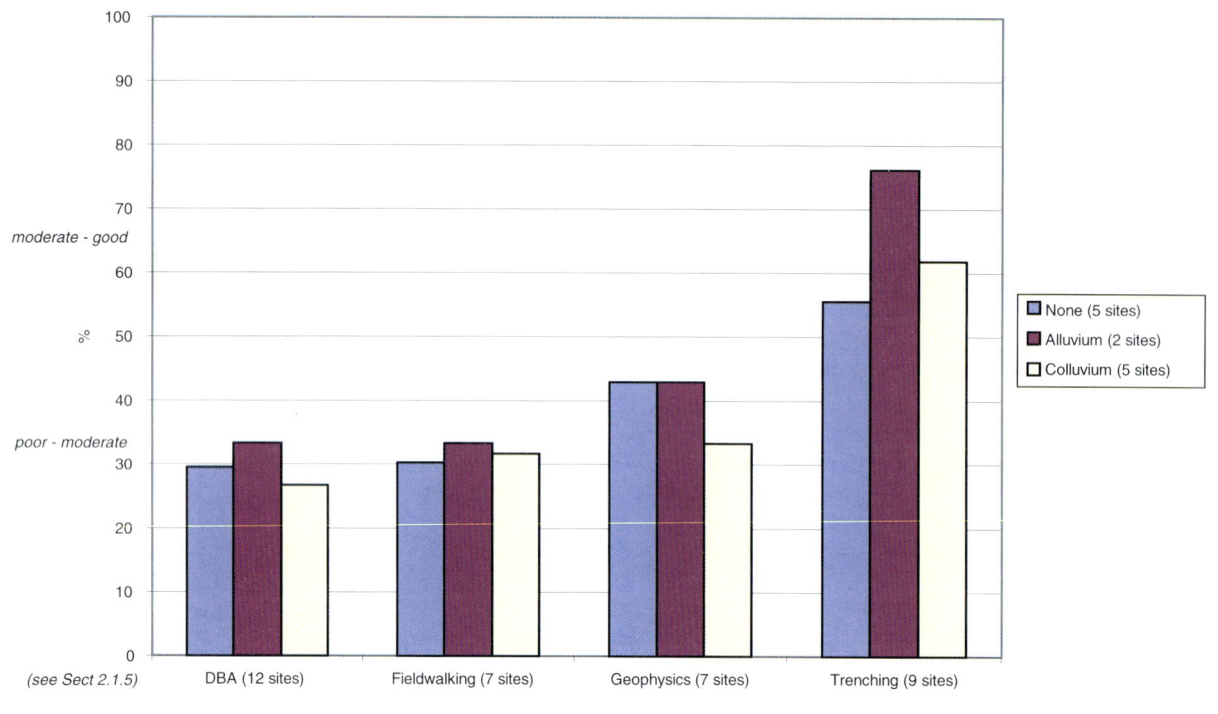

Figure 7 Success of techniques in relation to colluvium/alluvium

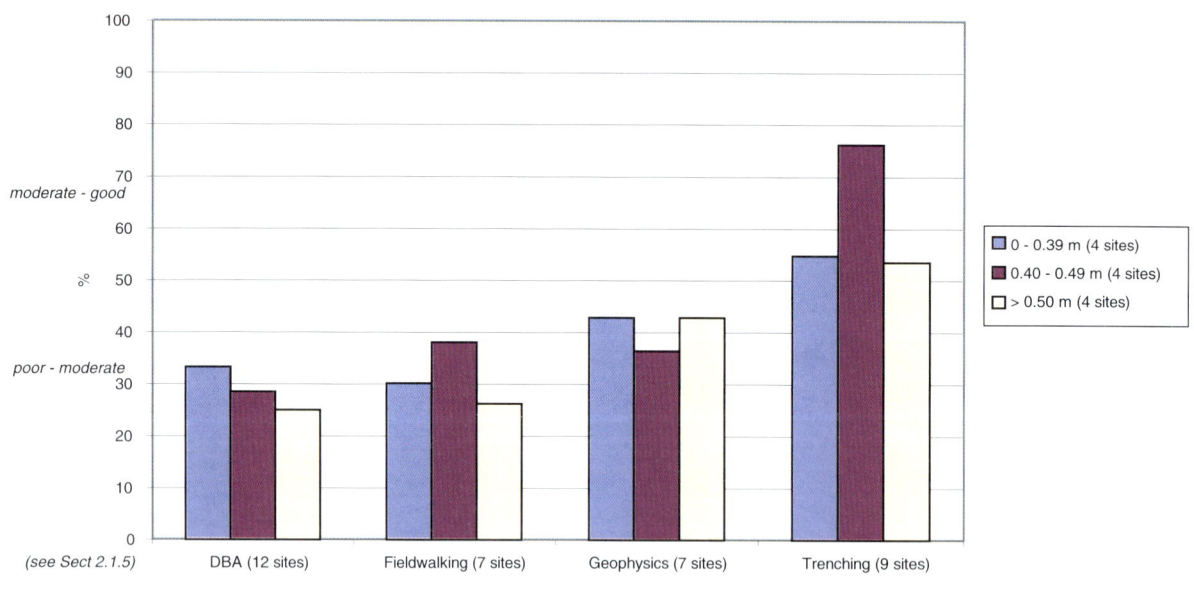

Figure 8 Success of techniques in relation to depth of overburden

remains had the most consistent correlation between depth of site and the success of the technique, with deeper sites providing the greatest impediment to discovery.

3.2.6 Recent land use

As the majority of sites (nine) had been arable to some extent before development and two were a mixture of arable and pasture, little can be said about the relative ease with which different techniques may have been undertaken as a result of different land-use histories. Geophysics was most successful on the only site that was purely pasture (Elms Farm) and, self-evidently, fieldwalking on arable sites (Fig. 9).

20

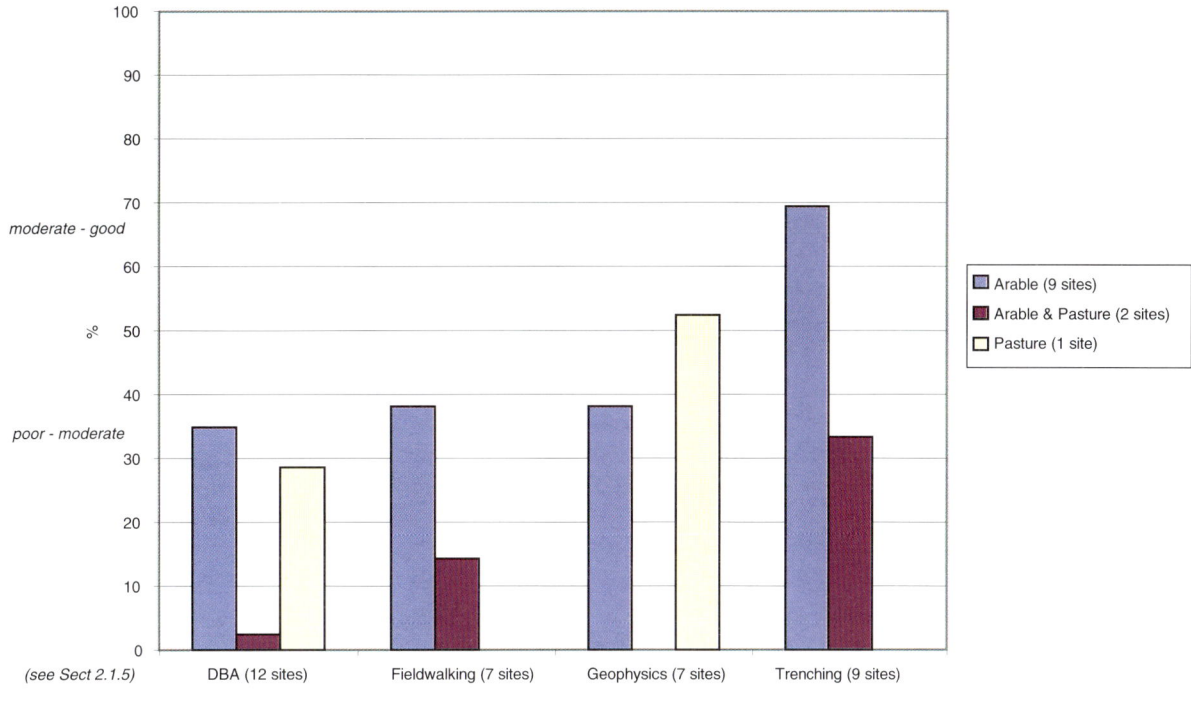

100
90
80
70
moderate - good
60
%
50
poor - moderate
40
30
20
10
0

□ Arable (9 sites)
■ Arable & Pasture (2 sites)
□ Pasture (1 site)

(see Sect 2.1.5)   DBA (12 sites)   Fieldwalking (7 sites)   Geophysics (7 sites)   Trenching (9 sites)

Technique

Figure 9 Success of techniques in relation to recent land use

3.2.7   Weather and ground conditions

The weather and ground conditions during evaluations can have an impact on the effectiveness of the exercise. Obviously, it is difficult to spot finds on the surface of a field if it is very dark or the crop is high. Fieldwalking took place between October and May on the projects in this study and, where conditions were noted, these seem to have been fair. The geophysical surveys (on seven projects) were undertaken throughout the year and, although the weather was not ideal during all of these, for example some of the surveys at Yarnton, this was not believed to have affected the results. Trench evaluations were also conducted at all times of year (February to November), but only for the work at Westhawk Farm were the adverse conditions (very wet with flooded trenches) felt to have an impact on the results. Several excavators commented that some features only became visible after trenches had been open for some time, raising concerns about what may be missed during the inevitable speed of most evaluation exercises. They did not feel, however, that this had affected seriously the outcome of the evaluation.

3.3   The success of different techniques

3.3.1   Desk-based assessment

Desk-based assessment was undertaken for all the projects in this study. For all sites and all periods it performed only poorly to moderately well (Fig. 10). It was most effective where previous work had been carried out in the immediate area, for example at Thurnham Roman villa and Thanet Way, and the presence of cropmarks also contributed to the more successful assessments, as at Northumberland Bottom.

The analysis showed that desk-based assessments were somewhat better at evaluating Roman and medieval sites, than those of the Neolithic, Bronze Age, Iron Age and early medieval/Anglo-Saxon periods, for which they performed poorly. Nevertheless, for the Anglo-Saxon period this form of evaluation was one of the most successful techniques.

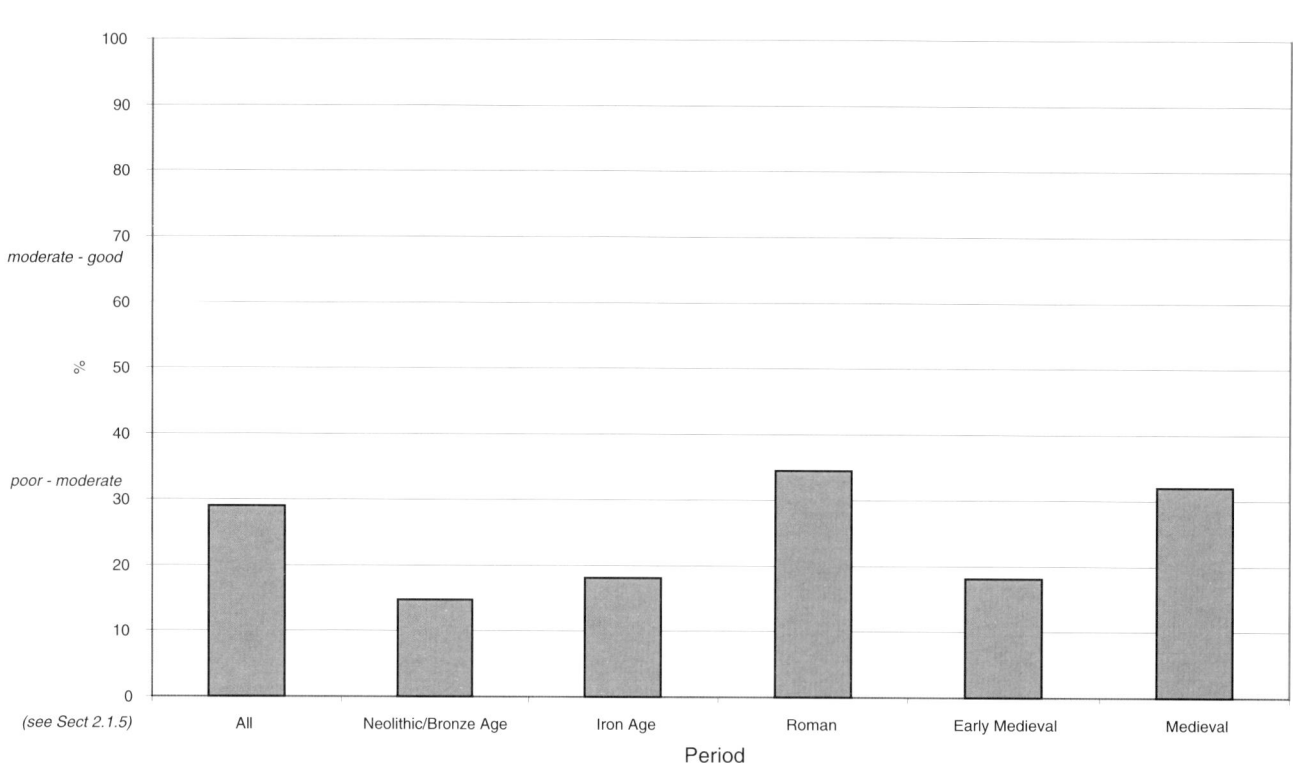

Figure 10 Success of desk-based assessment by period

Desk-based assessment was much better at indicating the presence of sites than it was at showing their precise location, intensity and character. It was very inadequate at revealing anything about layout, condition and quality of finds. Any scores it made here were the result of some previous knowledge derived from adjacent excavations.

It should be noted that these projects included some of the most thorough desk-based assessments undertaken, for the Environmental Assessment of the CTRL route was meticulous. In addition, two of the projects followed the line of previous linear schemes (Thurnham and Thanet Way) and so the depth of knowledge about likely remains was considerably greater that might be the case ordinarily. Hence desk-based assessments may have scored more highly here than would have been the average nationally.

3.3.2   *Fieldwalking*

Fieldwalking was conducted on seven of the projects in this study (Table 3). On six of these the collection units were the same (transects 20 m apart with finds bagged every 20 m), although a more intensive collection policy was subsequently adopted by Framework Archaeology at Stansted. A less-structured, walkover survey was conducted on the Whitfield to Eastry Bypass. The relative merits of different fieldwalking methodologies cannot, therefore, be assessed by this study.

Fieldwalking was only poor to moderate at evaluating these sites, although it performed slightly better than desk-based assessment (Fig. 11). An analysis by period shows that only for the Roman period was it moderately good as shown, for example, at Thurnham Villa (Fig. 12). Iron Age sites fared less well, although settlements at Stansted and Yarnton were both detected by these means (eg Fig. 13), but none of the Saxon sites found in these projects were detected by fieldwalking (only two of these sites were walked). For the Neolithic/Bronze Age, however, it was the most successful method used after machine trenching as, where remains are ephemeral but some artefacts are durable, fieldwalking can be a valuable technique. There should always be caution about assuming that scatters on the surface equate with sites beneath, as some false positives were recorded by this method. However, the scatters presumably related to sites that had been ploughed away showing that this technique can be extremely valuable for recording sites that would not be found by any other method except topsoil sieving (in test pits).

The general lack of success of fieldwalking, however, hides two important attributes of this method: indicating the presence of sites and suggesting their date. For these particular questions, fieldwalking produced good results, especially for the Neolithic/Bronze Age and Roman periods. It could also provide some information on precise location and intensity of activity, but it was very poor on issues of condition and layout of sites.

The ability to undertake fieldwalking depends on the presence of arable land, the proximity of the archaeological horizon to the modern surface and also the appropriate ground conditions for the period over which the evaluation must take place. In practice, this limits the applicability of this method.

3.3.3   *Metal detecting*

Metal detecting was used as a site-detection method over two of the sites which formed part of this study, Ramsgate Harbour Approach Road and Westhawk Farm. Only post-medieval finds were recovered at Ramsgate, but at Westhawk Farm metal finds very clearly indicated the presence of the Roman site, and the most intense area of activity within it (as supported by the geophysical survey). This technique was not integrated into the overall assessment of the success of

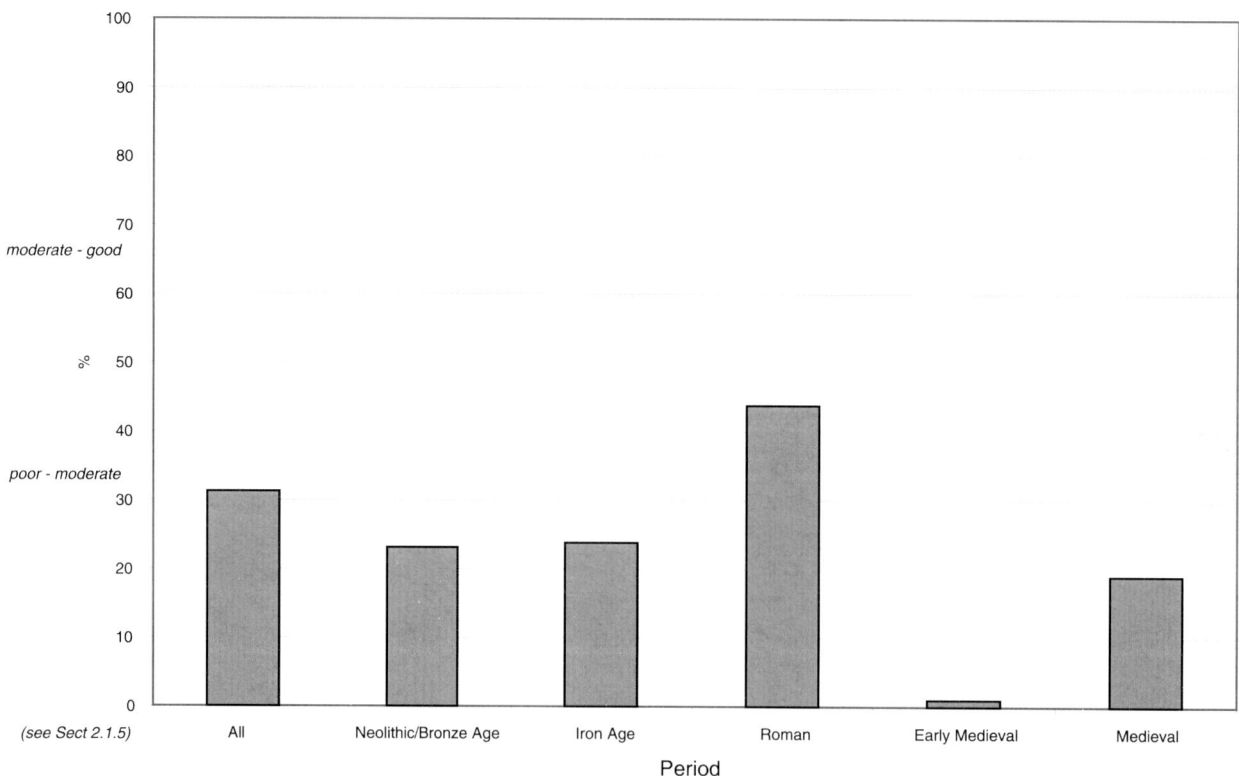

moderate - good

poor - moderate

(see Sect 2.1.5)

Period

Figure 11 Success of fieldwalking by period

24

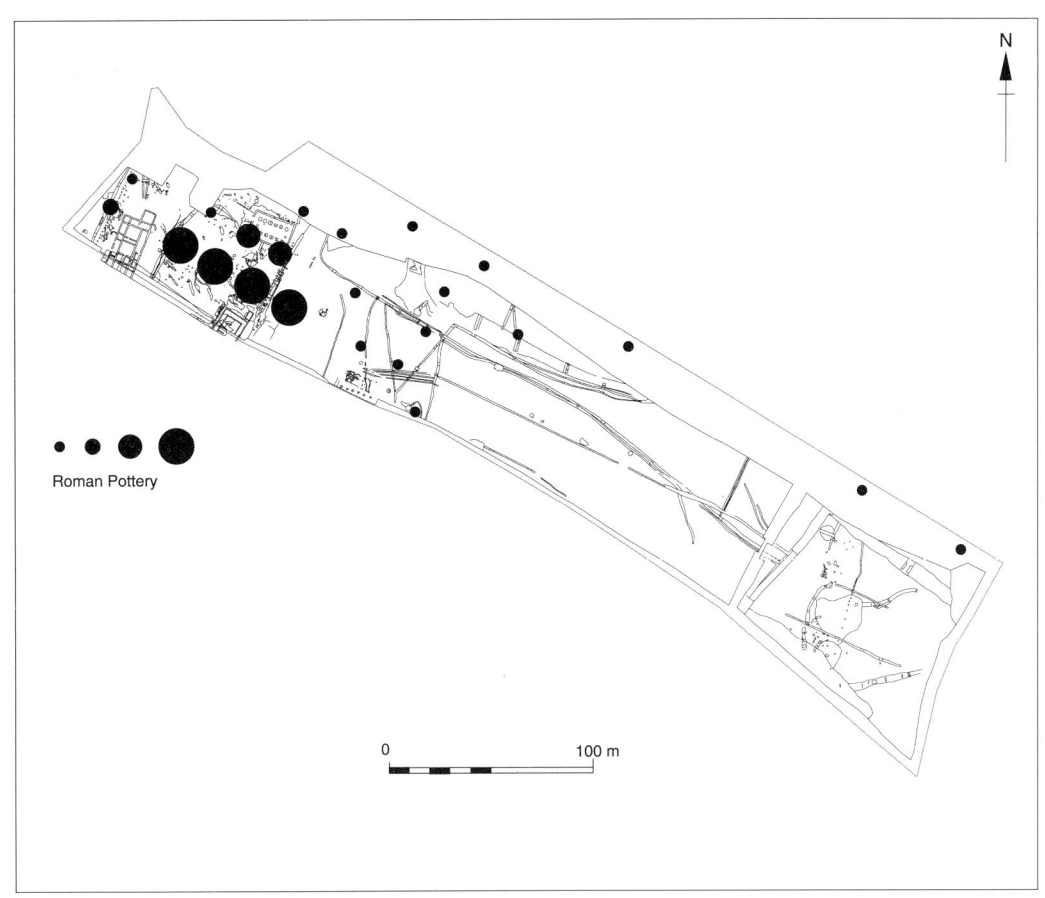

Figure 12 Fieldwalking at Thurnham Villa, Roman pottery

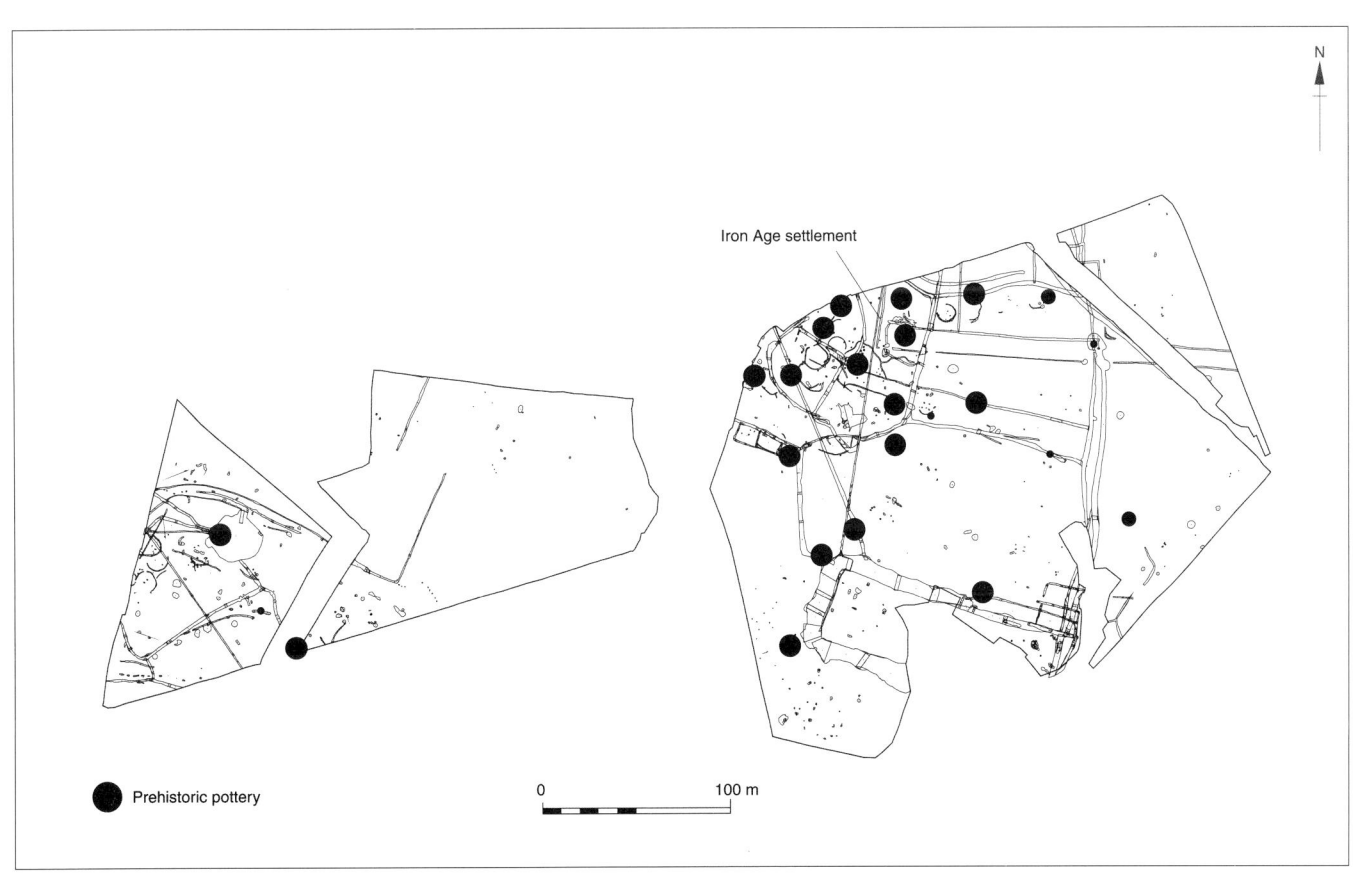

Figure 13 Fieldwalking at Stansted, Prehistoric pottery

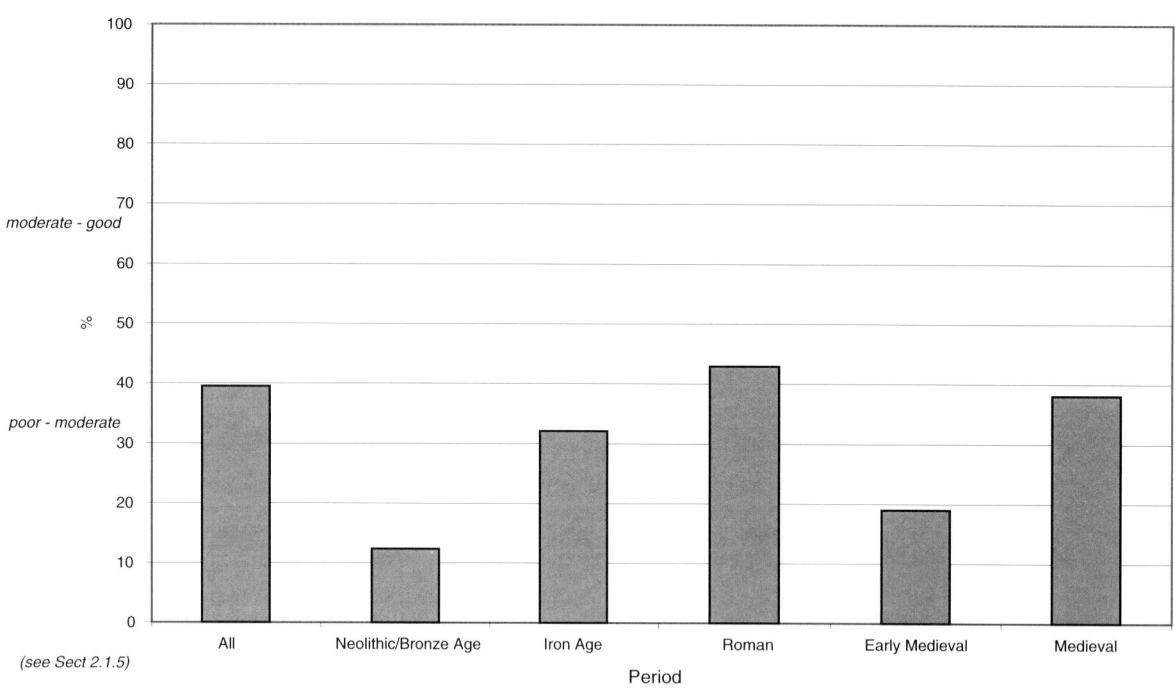

(see Sect 2.1.5)

Figure 14 Success of geophysical surveys by period

techniques but its potential use over sites of the Roman period was demonstrated. As with fieldwalking, it revealed no evidence for the condition and quality of buried remains, nor useful information on site layout.

3.3.4   Geophysical survey

Fluxgate gradiometer surveys were undertaken on seven sites in this study, with Twin Electrode resistance limited to one of these. Altogether, these techniques achieved a score that approached a moderately-good level for evaluating

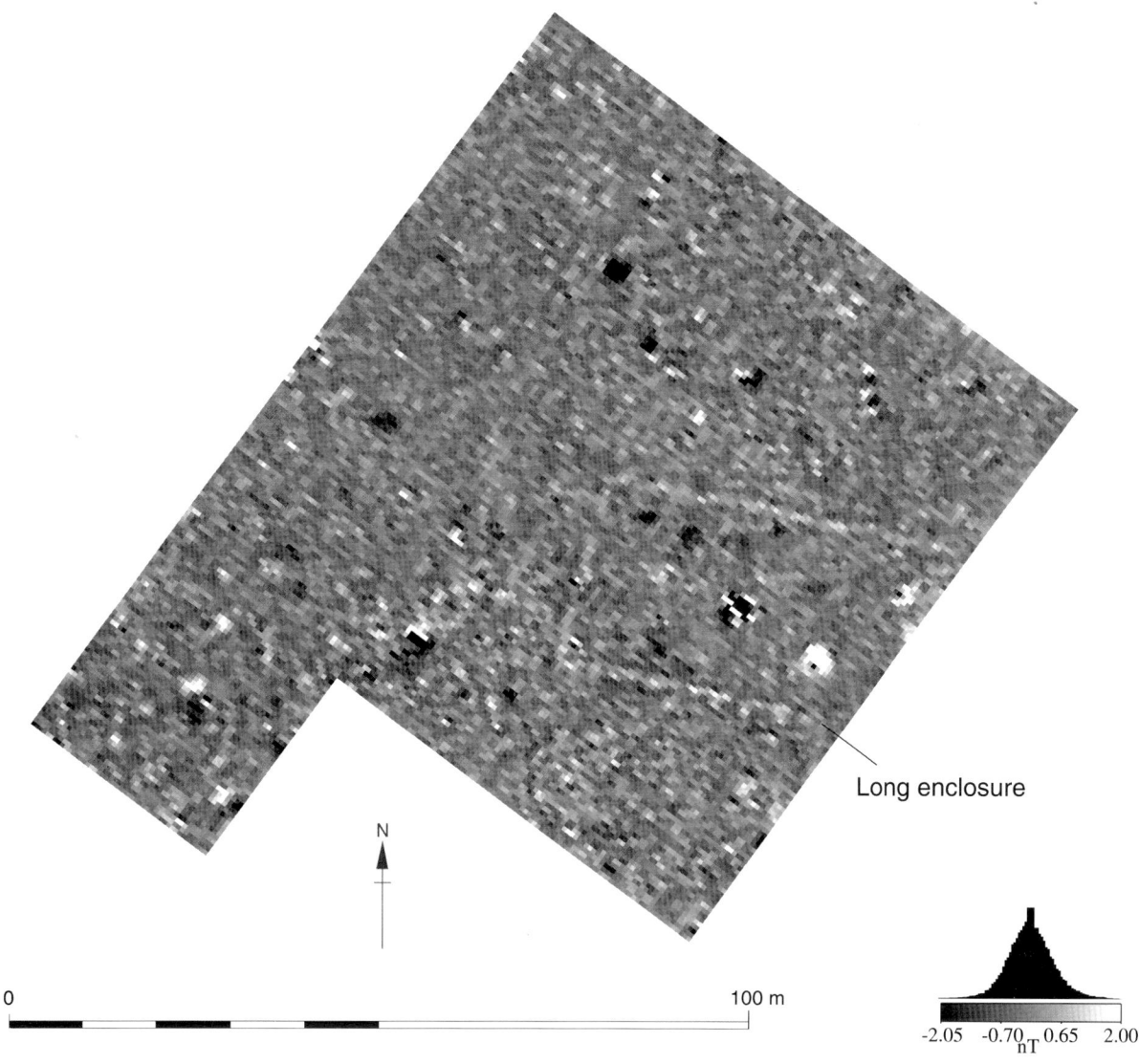

Long enclosure

N

0   100 m

-2.05 -0.70$_{nT}$ 0.65 2.00

Figure 15 Magnetometer survey at Yarnton Site 5

archaeological remains (Fig. 14) but were, of course, much better at locating sites with more substantial features and enhanced soils, such as Roman and some Iron Age settlement sites, and medieval landscape features such as boundary ditches. The poor record of geophysical survey for evaluating Neolithic and Bronze Age remains masks its relative success at locating funerary monuments, for example ring ditches and long enclosures, even those buried beneath alluvium at Yarnton (Figs 2 and 15). However, it was unable to detect any settlement remains for these periods. Similarly, most early medieval/Anglo-Saxon, and some later medieval settlement evidence was not found in geophysical survey. On the other hand, sunken-featured buildings which characterise many early Saxon sites were readily detected by these means at Yarnton, as they would probably have been at the other Saxon sites within this study, had geophysics been undertaken. It is noteworthy that the unusual sunken-featured buildings of Roman date on Thanet Way produced very strong anomalies, typical of the comparatively high magnetic enhancement for features of this period.

Where it was used, this method was good at indicating the presence of sites, and moderate to good at their precise location. It also was a moderately-good indicator of the density of features on a site, and by inference the date of the remains and it was the most successful evaluation technique for revealing site layout, even though it did not achieve such high scores for this aspect of evaluation. However, its success is only relative and it must be remembered that it was not

Temple

Figure 16 Excavated features at Westhawk Farm

good at finding some kinds of features, such as settlement evidence comprising largely posthole structures. Even within the Roman site of Westhawk, some important Roman features were not detected, including a small Roman temple (compare Figs 16 and 17). Geophysics could provide some indication of the condition of features (more than any other non-intrusive technique), but it was nevertheless poor at this and, of course, could not judge the quality of the artefactual remains in features.

These results were achieved by visual inspection and comparison of the geophysical surveys and final site plans by a non-specialist. More detailed analysis of surveys on five sites was conducted by Archaeometry Branch of the English Heritage Centre for Archaeology (Appendix 2).

3.3.5 Boreholes and test pits

Boreholes and test pits were only dug on four of these projects, Ramsgate Harbour Approach Road, Tutt Hill, White Horse Stone and Yarnton, and they were excavated for different purposes at each. At Tutt Hill the pits were dug for geotechnical purposes, but under archaeological observation; the presence of archaeological remains was indicated first by these means. At Ramsgate Harbour lithostratigraphic sections were examined in most of the evaluation trenches and additional boreholes were dug to supplement

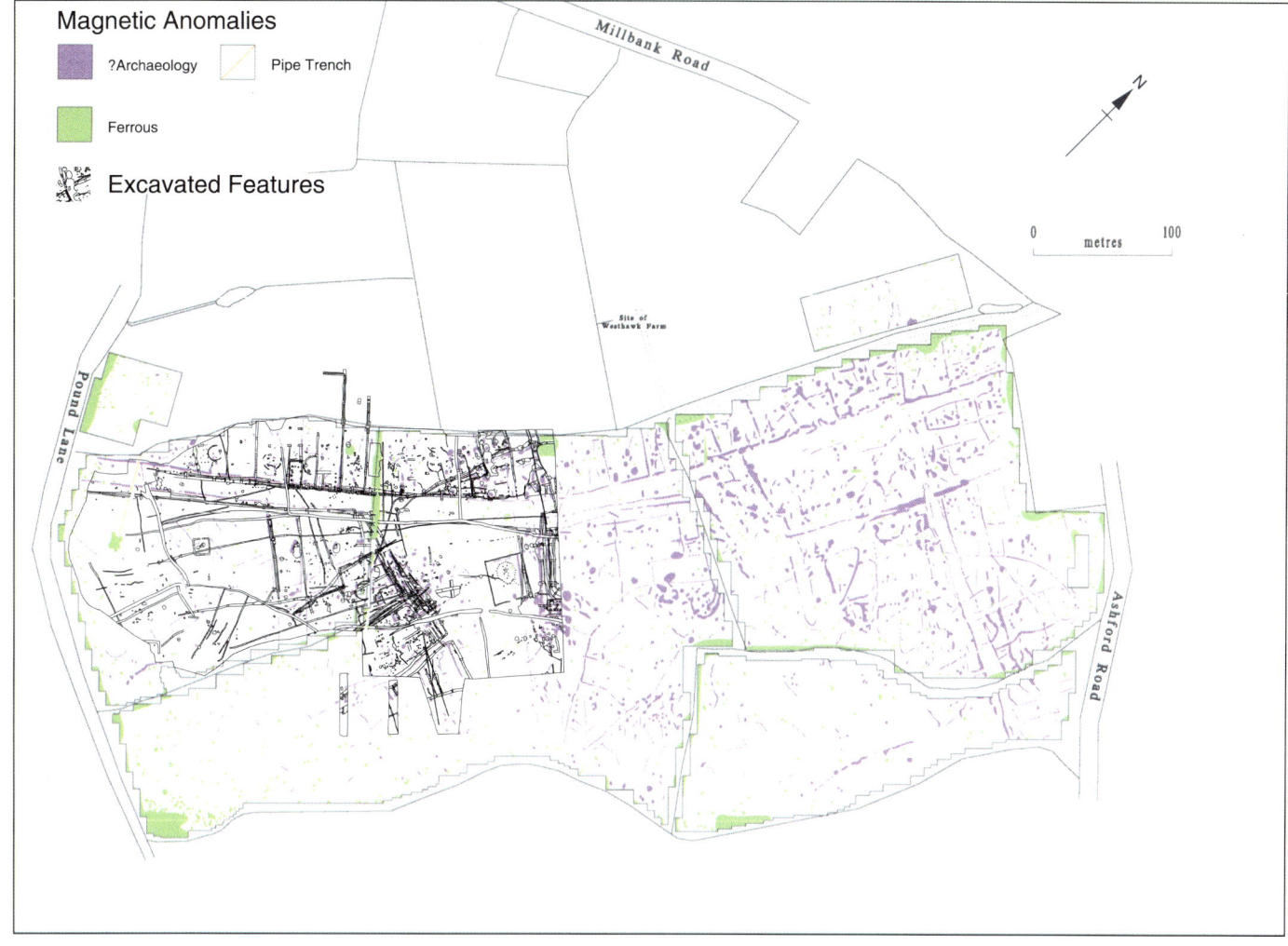

Magnetic Anomalies

?Archaeology   Pipe Trench

Ferrous

Excavated Features

Figure 17 Geophysical survey results overlain on excavated features at Westhawk Farm

these, to enable geoarchaeologists to investigate potential occupation surfaces at different levels within colluvial build-up. Test pits at White Horse Stone were dug for a similar purpose. None of the above work incorporated soil sieving. At Yarnton, 1 m x 1 m test pits were dug by hand and soil was sieved in order to understand and date soil build-up since the Neolithic period.

On none of these projects were boreholes or test pits used as a site detection method and, for this reason, they are not assessed with other methods used. It should be noted, however, that the simulations showed that pits performed poorly at locating archaeological sites; it was all too easy, even within a moderately-densely occupied Roman site, to miss virtually all features, and it could be extremely difficult to recognise those exposed in such small areas. Assessing layout, condition and quality of finds within features, as well as characterising sites, would all fare poorly by this method. Sieving soil obviously mitigates these problems to some extent, and may reveal information on the extent of post-depositional disturbance and the date of remains that once survived on the site. It may have advantages over fieldwalking in some circumstances where remains are more deeply buried and, obviously, in areas of pasture, but it is very hard to envisage a situation where test pits out-perform machine trenching. Nevertheless, sieving pits at the end of such trenches can be a very valuable exercise for evaluating post-depositional disturbance and dating build-up.

3.3.6   Machine trenching

Machine trenching was, after desk-based assessment, the most commonly employed evaluation method on these projects, and was used on eleven of the twelve

29

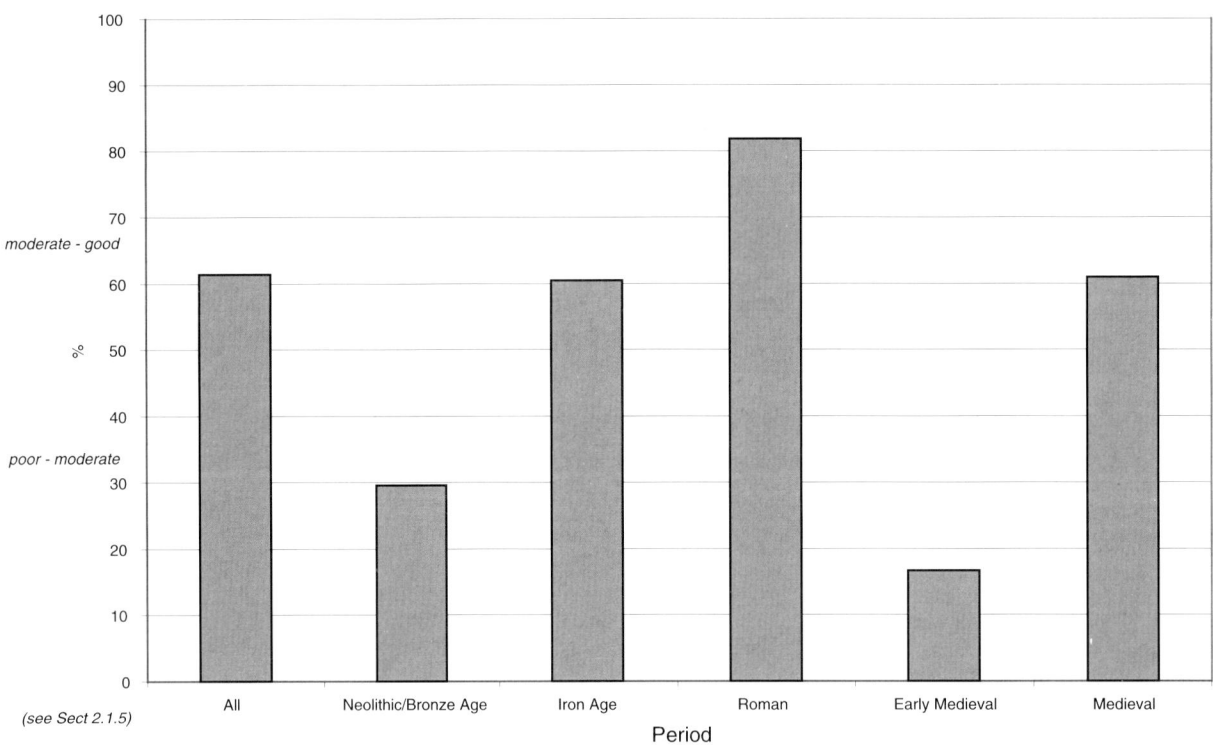

(see Sect 2.1.5)

Figure 18 Success of machine trenching by period

projects. It is the most common method of evaluation across England, very often being the only technique applied, and the results of this assessment demonstrate why this should be (Fig. 18). It was the only method that was moderate to good at evaluating these archaeological sites. However, it was significantly better at finding and assessing Roman (Fig. 19), Iron Age and medieval sites than those of the other periods, where its success was only moderate to poor or poor. The presence of a

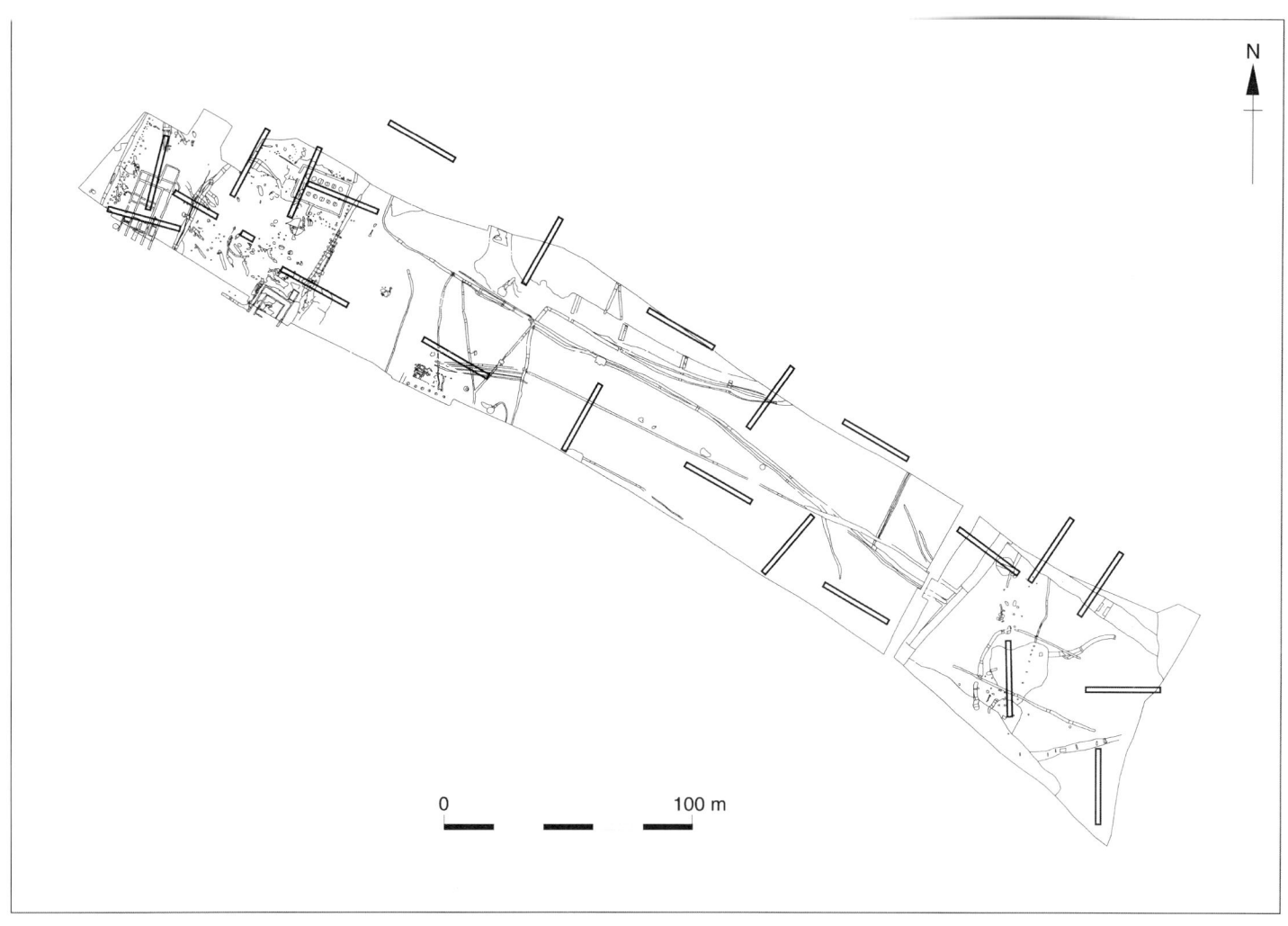

Figure 19 Thurnham Villa, actual trenching (3%)

linear component within sites of these periods seems to be a significant element in their detectability. For the Neolithic and Bronze Age trenching was the most successful method but it was only a marginal improvement on fieldwalking. This is a direct reflection of the problems of finding dispersed remains; for early medieval/Anglo-Saxon remains, it actually fared less well than desk-based assessment and geophysical survey. Trenches can be placed within a Saxon site and easily miss features because of the irregularity of their layout and the wide spaces between them, as they did in three out of the four cases within the study where Saxon features were later discovered. Geophysical survey can detect Anglo-Saxon sites if sunken-featured structures are present, but middle and later Saxon settlements, where sunken-featured buildings are less common are correspondingly more difficult to find.

Trenching was considerably better at indicating the presence of sites than it was at revealing other information about them, but it was the only technique which adequately indicated the condition of the remains and the quality of the artefacts and ecofacts present. It was moderately good at dating and characterising the archaeological remains and also at providing data on precise location of remains and intensity, although it was not significantly better than fieldwalking or geophysics for the last two questions (for the sites on which these techniques were undertaken). Geophysics was more effective at revealing site layout. However, machine trenching was, or could be, undertaken on all these sites, regardless of whether they had been ploughed or were receptive to geophysical survey.

At the Ramsgate Harbour Approach Road project, three phases of trenching were carried out, and this was felt to be valuable in enabling the results of the earlier stages to inform the strategies of the later phases of work. At Yarnton, a project with one of the most successful trenching exercises, provision was made for additional trenches to supplement the standard grid layout in order to follow up particular lines of investigation raised in the field. This strategy seems to have had a significant impact on the success of the exercise. Although these examples provide only anecdotal evidence, they suggest that such strategies are worthy of serious consideration.

3.3.7 Combining techniques

None of the projects examined in this study employed a single method of evaluation, and there is no doubt that combinations of techniques can provide very powerful tools for evaluating archaeological sites which far outweigh the sum of their individual values. Evaluation trenching designed to examine features and apparent gaps in the geophysical surveys at Thanet Way, Westhawk Farm and Elms Farm are obvious examples. Each technique provides slightly different kinds of information about the sites and landscapes present. At Yarnton, fieldwalking was the method which detected prehistoric activity on the floodplain, without which no further work would have been undertaken, but it was only a combination of geophysical survey and trenching that revealed the character and range of the sites present, and justified subsequent excavation. Geophysical survey alone would have produced only two, earlier prehistoric funerary sites.

A suite of methods will probably be appropriate for larger projects with more diverse physical conditions but, unfortunately, the number of projects examined in this study was too few and the combinations of techniques too diverse to draw any valid overall conclusions about the most effective combinations in different circumstances.

3.3.8 Strip, map and sample

Although not used explicitly as an evaluation method, two projects in this study undertook widespread stripping as an alternative to more detailed evaluation methods. On the Thanet Way project only limited trenching was undertaken in advance of stripping, and at Stansted a decision was taken to move straight to stripping following fieldwalking and very limited geophysical survey. An analysis of the practical value and cost-effectiveness of the Stansted approach will be undertaken by Framework Archaeology, and the strip-map-and-sample strategy is discussed generally below (Section 5.2). Ephemeral archaeological remains were detected on both sites which would have been hard, if not impossible to detect by other means (as shown by the simulated trenches). Stripping provides absolute certainty about the surviving archaeological evidence, but this must be balanced against the cost of exposing large areas (under archaeological supervision) where no archaeological features were present (see below).

3.4   Assessing different aspects of the archaeological remains

Presence. All techniques had some success in detecting the presence of sites within the development areas. Of these, trenching was the most effective, but fieldwalking and geophysical survey also performed well.

Precise location. All techniques were less successful at precisely indicating the location of sites, rather than suggesting their presence. In these cases, geophysics did rather better than the other methods (as used on seven sites).

Intensity and complexity of archaeological remains. This question was most effectively revealed by geophysics, although trenching also fared comparatively well.

Character of archaeological remains. Machine trenching was the most successful method for revealing the character of sites, but desk-based assessment was nearly as effective. However, no technique was more than moderately good.

Layout of buried archaeological remains. Perhaps unsurprisingly, geophysical survey was the most effective method for predicting site layout for all periods of archaeology on site, for those areas to which it was applied.

Condition of buried archaeological remains. Trenching was the only technique which adequately addressed the condition of buried remains, although geophysical survey did suggest survival to some extent.

Quality of artefacts and ecofacts in surviving archaeological remains. Only trenching was able to assess this issue, and its success was only moderate.
Date. Fieldwalking was the most successful technique for indicating the date of sites; sampling within machine trenches is notoriously weak at retrieving datable finds. Geophysical survey can only date features by inference.

False presence of sites. There were few instances of techniques indicating the presence of sites which were subsequently found not to survive. This was most likely to occur in fieldwalking. There were two examples (at Thurnham Villa and White Horse Stone) where flint and burnt stone clusters did not correspond to sub-soil features. This suggests that sites may once have been present, but had been ploughed away. In these cases it could be suggested that fieldwalking is positively misleading in the decision-making process, but the investigation of disarticulated sites within the ploughsoil is an issue that development-control officers may wish to pursue.

Identification of remains. Archaeological remains within trenches can be misidentified or not detected. This was not common, but occurred predominantly on brickearth geologies, or on those sites where archaeological horizons were difficult to identify. In all cases, the archaeologists recognised the potential problem and the subsequent mitigation took this factor into account.

4 RESULTS: COMPUTER SIMULATIONS

4.1 Comparison between the trench arrays

The trench and pit arrays selected for simulation are shown on Figure 20, and several are illustrated on Figures 21-22 and 24-5. The sites to which they were applied, and the sample fractions assessed are shown in Table 5, and the results for all simulations are provided in Appendix 3 (Tables A3.1-6).

4.1.1 Comparing standard grid and parallel arrays

Based on a commonly used trench layout plan, the first array assessed was a 'standard' arrangement of trenches in a grid pattern, where each trench was aligned at 90 degrees to the one adjacent to it. The trenches were 30 m long and 2 m wide (Fig. 20, Array 1 and Fig. 21). This was compared with an arrangement of trenches of the same size where all were on the same alignment, with the rows offset to achieve a staggered layout of parallel trenches (Fig. 20, Array 4, and Fig. 22). This kind of array is commonly employed in mainland Europe.

Simulations of these arrays were undertaken for all the sites except Elms Farm (for the reasons discussed above, Section 2.3), at trench sample fractions of 2%, 3%, 5%, and 10% (Table 5). On the Thurnham Villa, Northumberland Bottom and White Horse Stone sites they were also examined at 4%. The results are shown on Figure 23 (the means of arriving at these totals is described in Section 2.1.5).

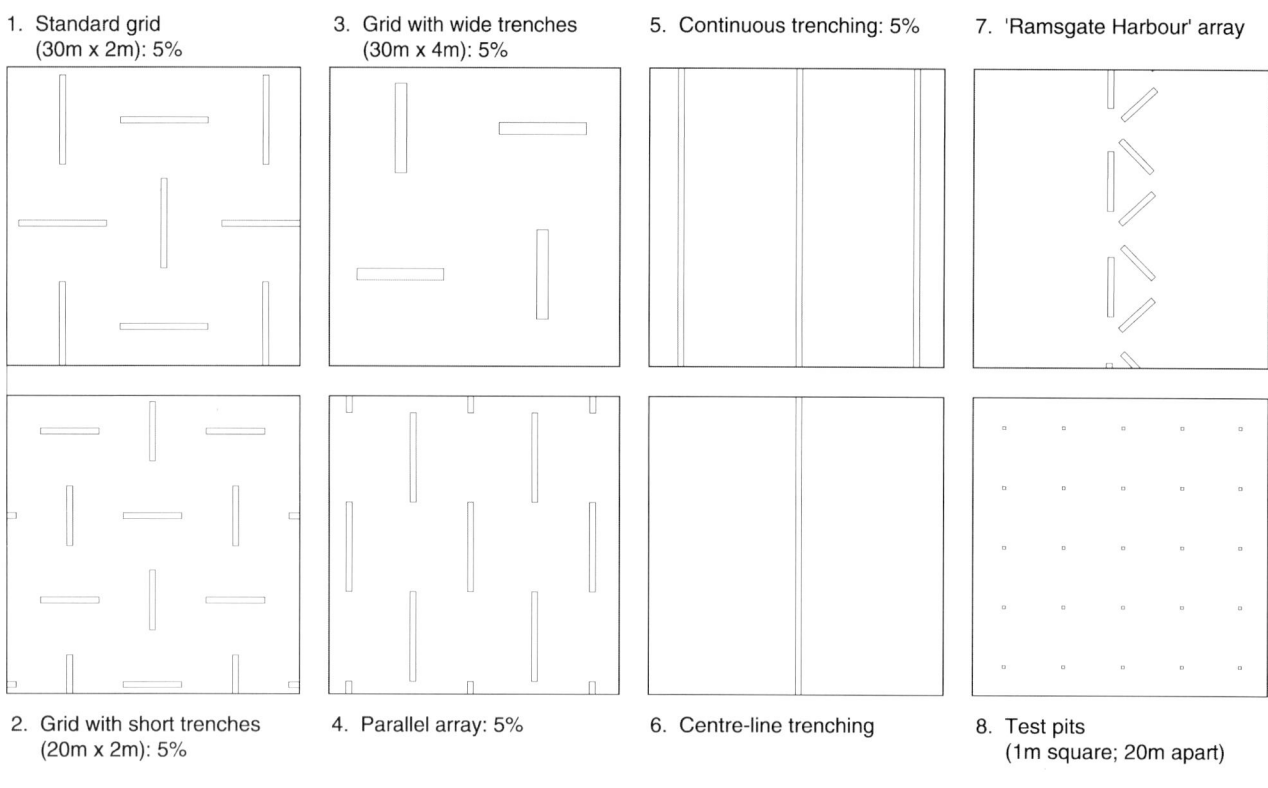

1. Standard grid
   (30m x 2m): 5%

2. Grid with short trenches
   (20m x 2m): 5%

3. Grid with wide trenches
   (30m x 4m): 5%

4. Parallel array: 5%

5. Continuous trenching: 5%

6. Centre-line trenching

7. 'Ramsgate Harbour' array

8. Test pits
   (1m square; 20m apart)

0   100 m

Figure 20 The simulated trench arrays

Table 5 Simulations undertaken

Array type	Sample fraction	Thurnham	Northumberland Bottom	White Horse Stone	Tutt Hill	Westhawk	Thanet Way	Ramsgate Harbour	Whitfield Eastry	Tesco Ramsgate	Elms Farm	Stansted	Yarnton Site 7
1. Standard grid (30mx2m)	2%	✓M*	✓	✓*	✓	✓*	✓*	✓	✓	✓*		✓*	✓*
	3%	✓M*	✓	✓*	✓	✓*	✓*	✓	✓	✓*		✓*	✓*
	4%	✓M*	✓	✓*									
	5%	✓M*	✓12	✓12*	✓	✓*	✓*	✓	✓	✓*		✓*	✓*
	10%	✓*	✓	✓*	✓	✓*	✓*	✓	✓	✓*		✓*	✓*
2. Grid with short trenches (20mx2m)	2%	✓M	✓	✓									
	3%	✓M	✓	✓									
	4%	✓M	✓	✓									
	5%	✓M	✓	✓									
	10%	✓	✓	✓									
3. Grid with wide trenches (30mx4m)	2%	✓	✓	✓									
	3%	✓	✓	✓									
	4%	✓	✓	✓									
	5%	✓	✓	✓									
	10%	✓	✓	✓									
4. Parallel array	2%	✓M	✓	✓	✓	✓	✓	✓	✓	✓		✓	✓
	3%	✓M	✓	✓	✓	✓	✓	✓	✓	✓		✓	✓
	4%	✓M	✓	✓									
	5%	✓	✓	✓	✓	✓	✓	✓	✓	✓		✓	✓
	10%	✓	✓	✓	✓	✓	✓	✓	✓	✓		✓	✓
Continuous trenching	2%	✓	✓	✓				✓					
	3%	✓M	✓	✓									
	4%	✓	✓	✓									
	5%	✓M	✓	✓									
	10%	✓M	✓	✓									
6. Centre-line trenching		✓	✓	✓			*						
7. 'Ramsgate Harbour' array		✓	✓	✓			*	✓					
8. Test Pits (1m square; 20m apart)		✓	✓	✓									
Actual Trenching			*	*		*	*			*		*	*

✓ Simulation undertaken

12 12 regularly-spaced simulations examined

M Maximum and minimum position examined

* Quantification undertaken

In terms of their performance at detecting archaeology of all periods, these two trenching strategies produced very similar results. In both cases the simulations at a sample fraction of 2% produced poor to moderate results, rising to moderate results for 3%, moderate to good results at 5%, and good results at 10% (see below, Section 4.2 and Fig. 31, where the increase of knowledge gained is compared to the increase in the number of trenches and cost). When examined in more detail it was revealed that, while the performance of these two techniques was comparable for archaeology of most types, for the generally easier to detect Roman and medieval periods the grid array performed consistently better than the parallel array, at all sample fractions. This is probably because of the higher component of linear features on sites of these periods which are more likely to be transected by the grid array.

4.1.2   *Comparisons with other arrays*

On three sites of very different character (Thurnham Villa, Northumberland Bottom and White Horse Stone) eight arrays were compared at 2%, 3%, 4%, 5% and 10% (Table 5). The Thurnham site was mainly Roman in date, with structures but also prehistoric elements, Northumberland Bottom had a strong linear component in sites of Bronze Age to medieval date, and White Horse Stone revealed mainly unenclosed Neolithic and Iron Age settlement remains. In addition to the two trench types discussed above, these simulations (illustrated on Fig. 20) comprised:

- a variation on the grid array using shorter trenches (20 m by 2 m in size) and, therefore, a greater number of sample units (Array 2)
- a third variation on the grid array using trenches of double the normal width (30 m x 4 m; eg Fig. 24), potentially improving the chances of identifying archaeological remains consisting of small or ephemeral features such as posthole structures (Array 3)
- a continuous trench system, based on sample fractions as with the other arrays, but in such a way that a number of relatively widely-spaced, unbroken lines were seen (Array 5)
- a modification of continuous trenching, examining a centre-line strip, 2 m wide (Array 6)
- a trench array based on the actual layout used for the Ramsgate Harbour Approach Road (Fig. 25), with a line of 20 m by 2 m trenches approximately 20 m apart, and an adjacent arrangement of 15 m by 2m trenches placed at an angle. This array (Array 7), which was designed for the particular topography of this site on the edge of a buried dry valley, was not arranged as a sample fraction (but at Ramsgate Harbour 5.6% was seen)
  test pits 1 m x 1m spaced at 20 m intervals (Array 8)

Only the results for the three sites on which all eight trench types were modelled are taken into account in the discussion that follows (see Table 6). However, it should be pointed out that the smaller number of sites means that the results are less reliable statistically than those where eleven sites are taken into account.

When considering effectiveness at detecting 'all archaeology', irrespective of period, the standard grid array of 30 m trenches performed reasonably well (Fig. 26). However, when the results are looked at by period, it is obvious (and perhaps unsurprising) that, whereas medieval and (to a slightly lesser extent) Roman remains are represented well by this method, the more ephemeral types of archaeology such as Neolithic and Bronze Age remains are actually poorly detected. Success in detecting Iron Age features lies between the two extremes (Table 6).

As in the comparison between all sites discussed above (Section 4.1.1), simulations using the parallel trenches on the three sites produced similar results to the

Table 6 Simulation results for different arrays for all archaeology and by period

Array Type	Sample Fraction	All Archaeology	Neolithic/Bronze Age	Iron Age	Roman	Medieval
1. Standard Grid (30m x 2m)	2%	38	11	36	39	58
	3%	49	14	53	69	78
	4%	66	50	44	72	75
	5%	66	25	56	75	92
	10%	93	81	81	92	94
2. Grid with short trenches (20m x 2m)	2%	33	8	14	44	22
	3%	56	17	39	58	61
	4%	67	36	58	75	75
	5%	76	36	69	86	89
	10%	93	81	81	92	94
3. Grid with wide trenches (30 x 4m)	2%	13	0	25	14	8
	3%	24	3	17	17	22
	4%	56	39	42	56	47
	5%	53	31	42	58	58
	10%	91	67	75	89	92
4. Parallel array	2%	27	8	17	31	36
	3%	51	11	44	58	50
	4%	76	72	61	81	64
	5%	73	36	64	72	78
	10%	96	83	92	92	92
5. Continuous trenching	2%	24	19	6	22	14
	3%	18	22	0	31	47
	4%	58	44	36	44	53
	5%	62	28	64	75	78
	10%	96	89	78	92	92
6. Centre-line trenching		42	25	28	39	56
7. 'Ramsgate Harbour' array		53	25	36	58	58
8. Test pits (1 metre square; 20m apart)		7	3	3	17	11

Scores out of 100

standard grid array (Array 4; Figs 23 and 26), although for these particular sites it produced poorer results at 2% and better results at 4%. As with Array 1, it was better at evaluating Roman and medieval remains than those of earlier periods (Table 6).

The grid array with shorter, and therefore more trenches produced very similar results in terms of its detection of archaeological remains as a whole (Array 2; Fig. 26). Thus the different trench-distribution pattern created by using more sampling units failed to improve detection rates, at least in these cases. There appeared to be little difference in this array's ability to detect Roman and medieval features, and it failed to result in an increased level of discovery for the harder to detect periods, but it appeared to be slightly poorer at identifying Iron Age remains at low percentages than the first array (Table 6).

The array designed with double-width trenches, so that each trench offered a larger area in which to identify features, was significantly less effective than the other 'grid' strategies and the parallel array, except at 10% when this technique did produce good results (Array 3; Fig. 26). This seemed to be a result of the correspondingly larger gaps between trenches. The harder to detect periods received particularly poor results, especially at the lower sample fractions (Table 6), but this array even performed badly for Roman and medieval archaeology, except at very high trench densities.

The simulations based on a number of long unbroken trenches (Array 5; 2 m in width, and continuing across the extent of the evaluation area) performed fairly poorly, with good results only achieved at higher percentages (Fig. 26). However, for the Neolithic and Bronze Age remains this technique was actually slightly more effective than the standard grid array at all percentage levels, except 4% (Table 6).

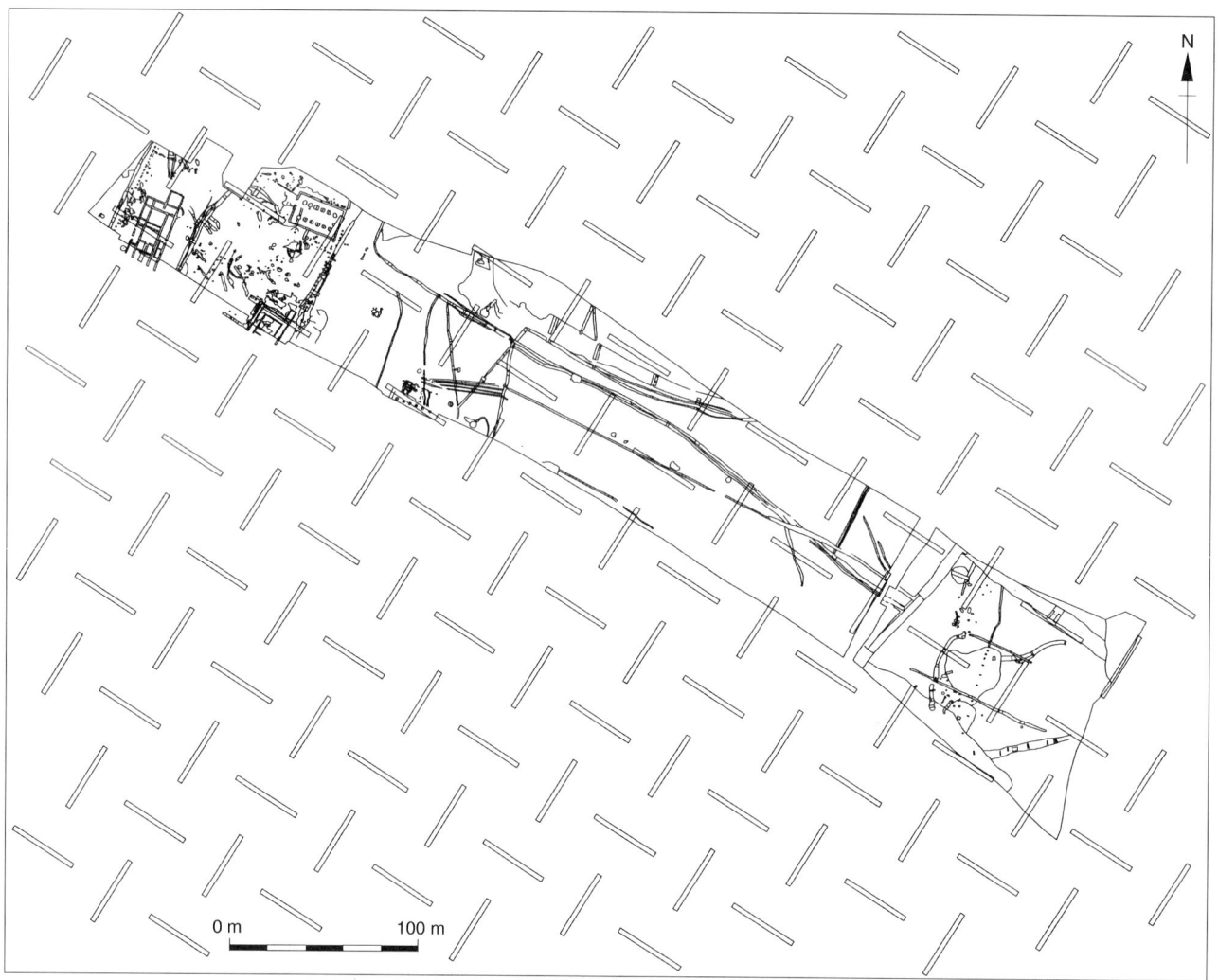

Figure 21 Thurnham Villa with 5% standard grid array

A single unbroken trench aligned along the centreline of an evaluation area produced a 'poor to moderate' performance across all periods, except medieval, where it achieved a moderate result (Array 6; Fig. 26; Table 6).

The experiments using the 'Ramsgate Harbour Approach Road' array displayed a moderate performance (Array 7; Fig. 26), with an expected degree of variation between the different periods. However, the best results (for medieval and Roman remains) could still be described only as moderate (Table 6). The actual results of trenching at Ramsgate were somewhat better than these (moderate to good), as the array was designed for the specific topographical circumstances of the site. This suggests that customised trench designs can be effective in some situations.

The simulations of test-pitting strategies all produced very poor results for detecting archaeology, for remains of all periods (Array 8; Fig. 26).

In conclusion, none of the arrays examined succeeded in demonstrating that they were significantly more successful than the standard grid array. Other arrays produced a comparable standard of results in certain circumstances, but these techniques were usually let down by their performance under other conditions. For example, the strategy based on a series of continuous trenches appeared to provide a marginally better performance at detecting Neolithic and Bronze Age remains than the grid array, but for other periods it performed badly, especially at lower sample fractions. Even the grid arrays with 20 m trenches (Array 2) and parallel trenches (Array 4), both of which produced equally good results at higher

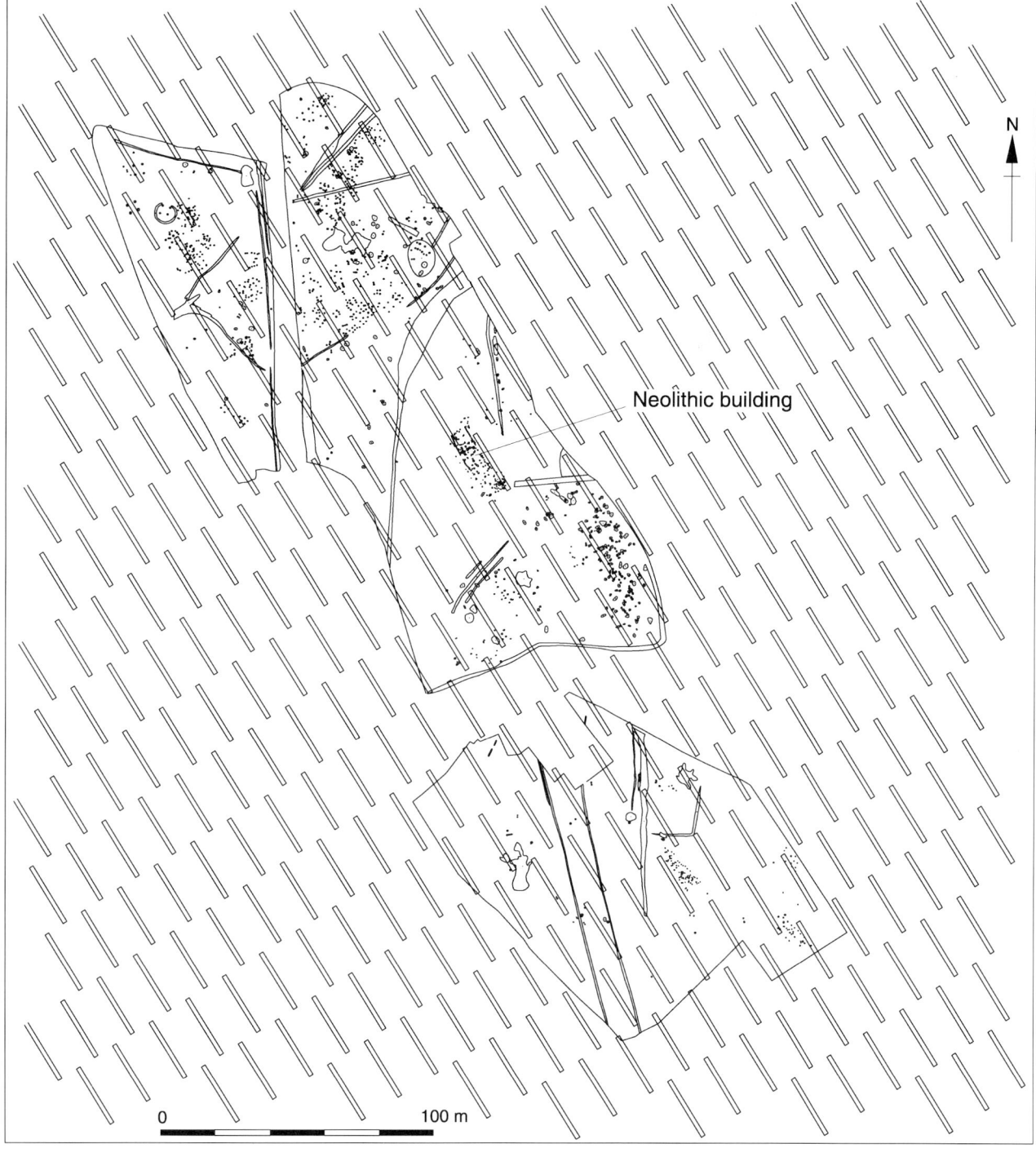

Figure 22 White Horse Stone with 10% parallel trenches

sample fractions, were less effective at 2% and 3%.

The results also suggest that some techniques should be used only with caution. For example, at anything but the 10% level the array using double-width trenches performed surprisingly poorly, especially for the harder to detect types of archaeology. The use of test pits at the concentrations modelled also seem to be a very poor means of identifying archaeological remains of any period.

Experiments, described below, looked at the best and worst possible positions of trench arrays at Thurnham Villa and reached similar conclusions to the results discussed above. However, they did demonstrate that, despite achieving a good result in an individual simulation, a particular array has the potential to perform very variably. For example, a simulation of 5% continuous trenching at Thurnham Villa gained a score of 11 (out of a possible 15 points), compared to the score of

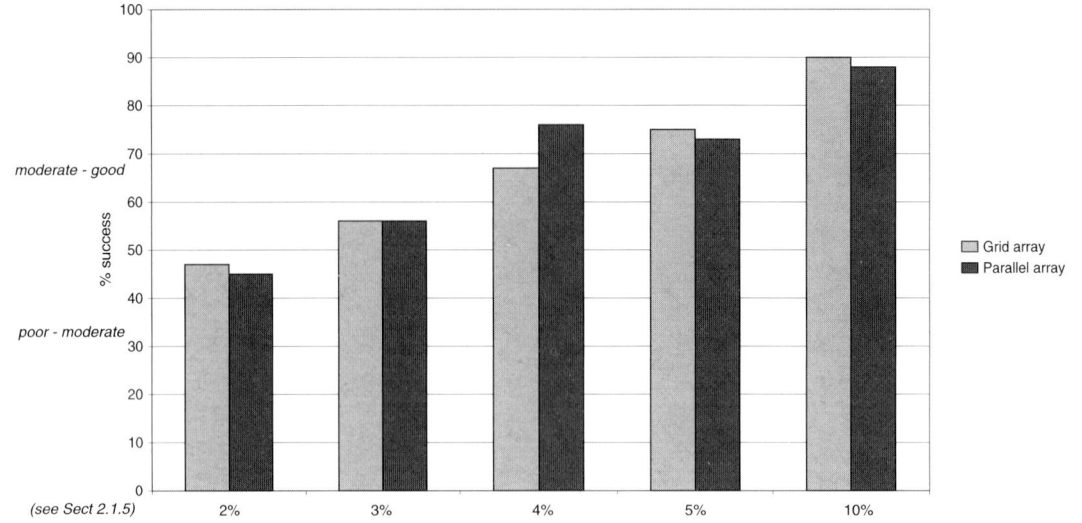

Figure 23 Comparison of success of standard grid and parallel trenches (Arrays 1 and 4)

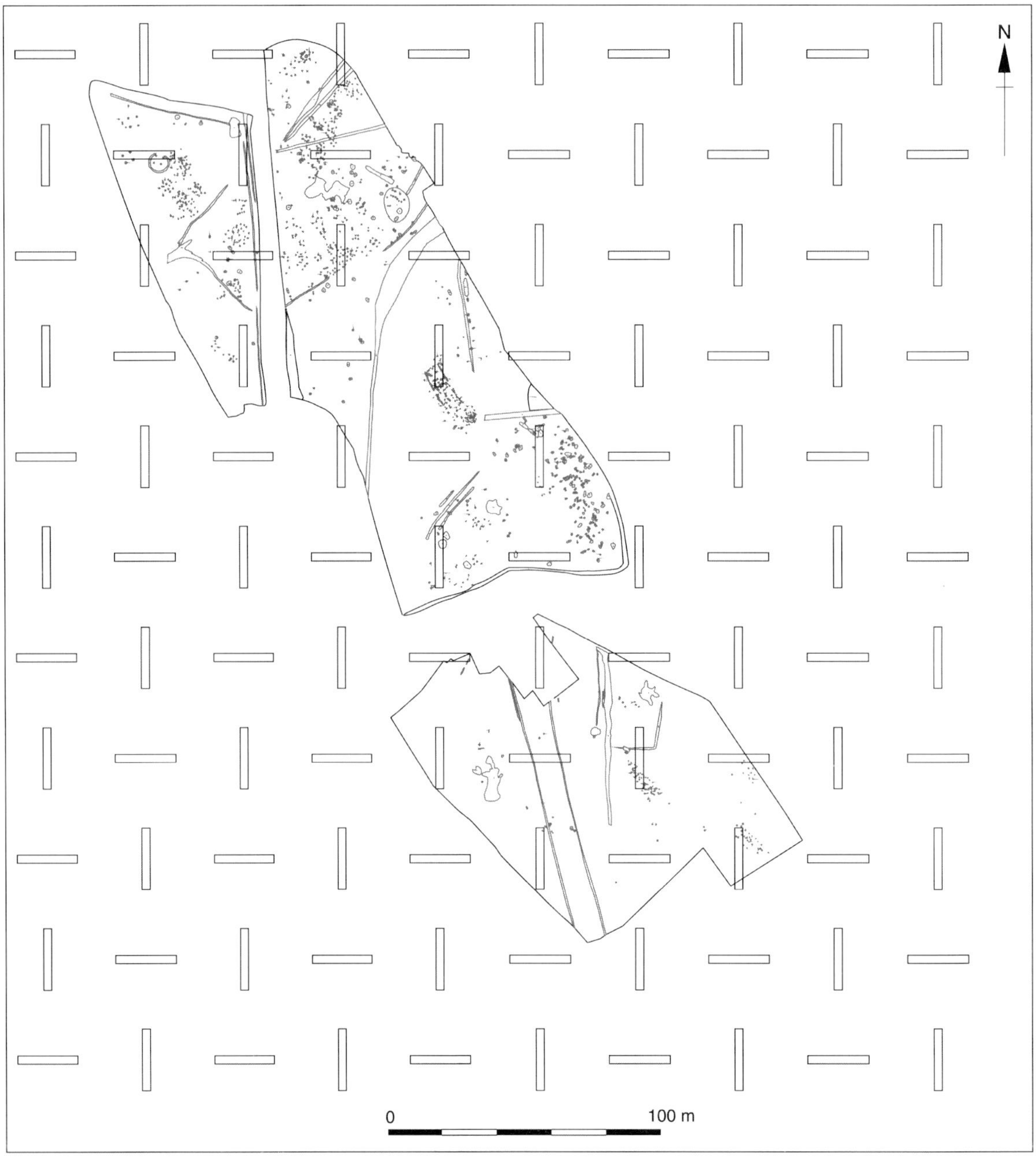

Figure 24 White Horse Stone with grid array of wide trenches

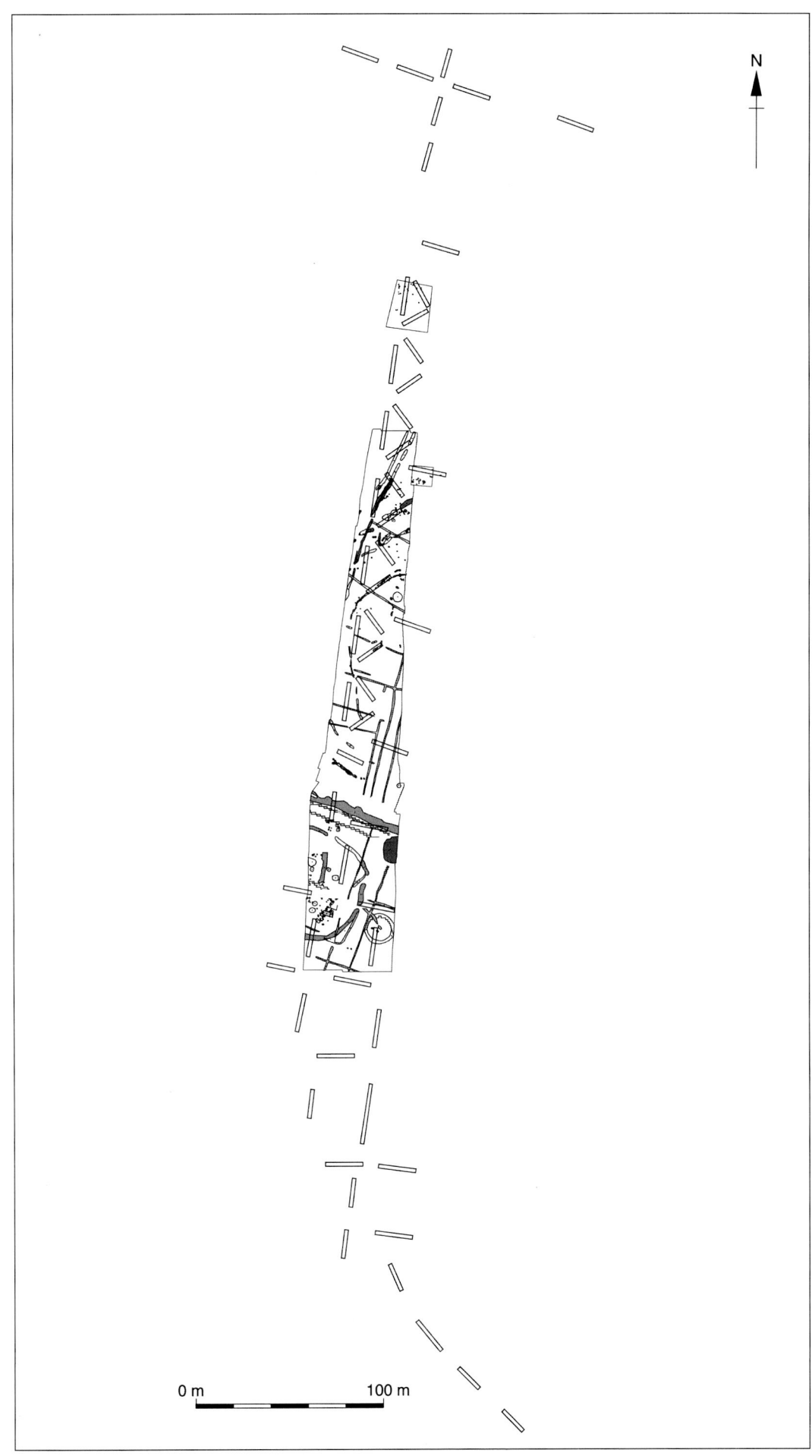

Figure 25 The 'Ramsgate Harbour' Array

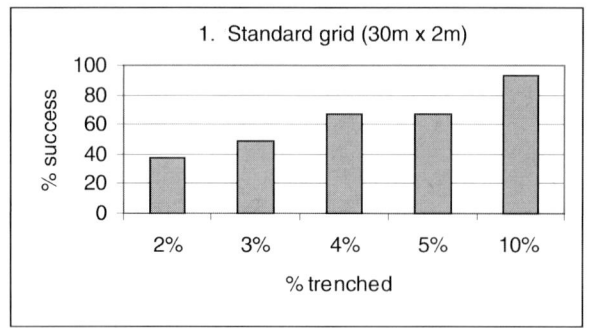

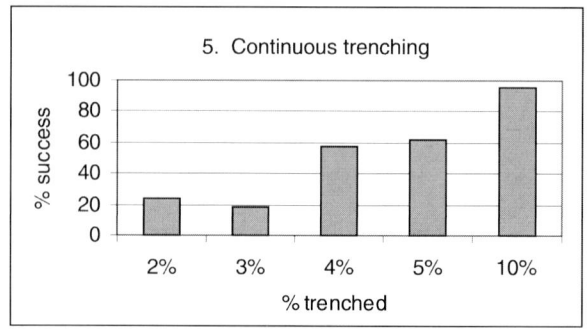

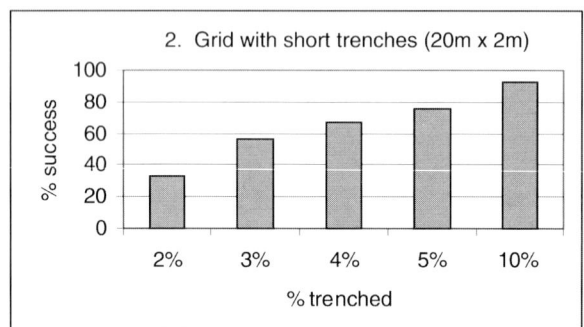

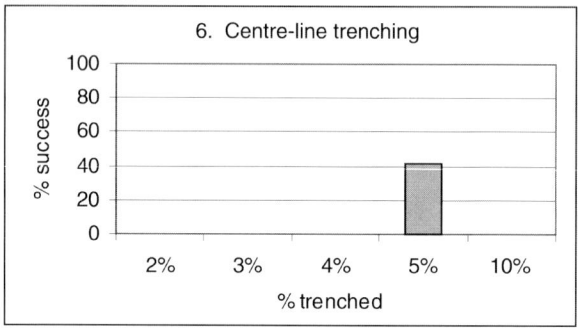

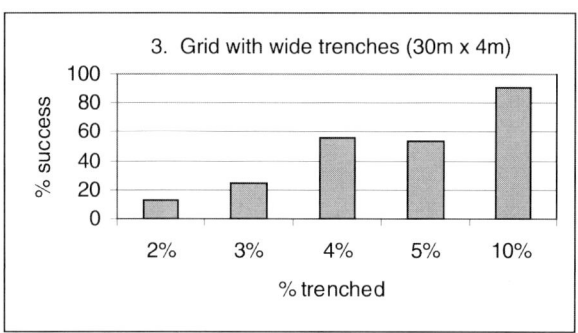

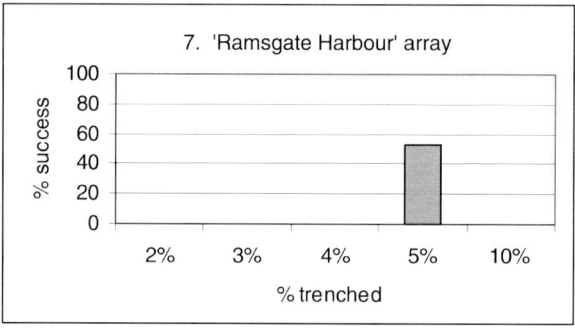

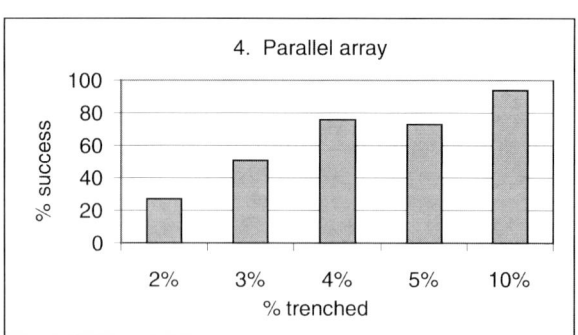

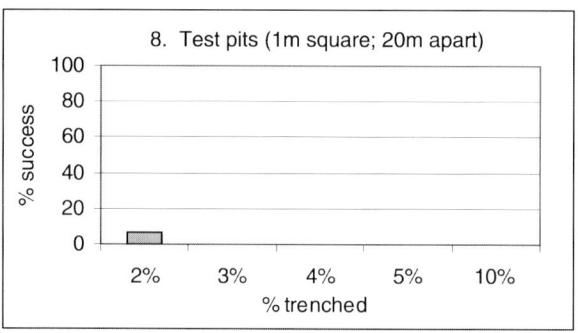

Figure 26 Comparative success of different trench arrays

10 achieved by the grid type array at the same percentage and that, whereas the standard grid array had a 'best possible' score of 12, the continuous trench strategy achieved a best result of 14 points (Table 8). Despite this, continuous trenching would appear to be a more risky strategy because (most importantly) the 'worst possible' result of the continuous trench method was 5 points, whereas the grid array gained 8 points.

4.2   Comparison between different sample fractions

In addition to looking at trench types and positions, a range of sample fractions was simulated for each trench type, as shown on Table 5, and this produced some interesting results. As expected, there was a general rise in effectiveness in a given trenching array as gradually increasing proportions of the evaluation area were seen. However, the increase in performance was not directly proportional to the actual increase in the total evaluation area trenched. Figure 27, using the standard grid array and the parallel array modelled on eleven sites, illustrates the curve showing the information gained as the number of trenches increased. This shows that, whereas there was a fairly constant rise in information gained from 2% to 5% as the sample fraction increased (with a small blip at 4%), the learning curve flattened considerably between 5% and 10%. Thus, the increased investment in effort (and cost) was not met, in general, by an equivalent increase in knowledge. For example, when the scores achieved by all the sites were combined for archaeology of all periods, and percentages of the maximum scores possible were calculated, the first grid array at 5% scored a result of 75%, while for the same array at 10% the result was 90% of the maximum. This increase is relatively modest, considering that the latter simulation had twice as many evaluation trenches. This pattern proved to hold true across the range of different trenching arrays tested, as judged on the three sites for which all eight designs were simulated.

When this situation was examined on a period by period basis, it was possible to discern some variation within the general trend. The periods which were easiest to detect (Roman and medieval) and which, therefore, usually scored well, produced least gain from increasing the sample fraction to high levels (Fig. 28). For example, for medieval archaeology (considering the grid array simulations on the eight sites containing remains of this date), as a percentage of the maximum score possible, the result for a 5% array was 89%, whereas doubling the number of trenches to create a 10% array only improved this result to 94%. Conversely, sites containing the harder to detect periods, such as Neolithic and Bronze Age, were more likely to benefit from using evaluation trenches at higher sample fractions (52% at a 5% sample to 85% at a 10% sample). Early medieval/Anglo-Saxon sites fared poorly in all these simulations and the greatest gain in knowledge, for the five projects where remains of this date were present, appeared to be between 3% and 5%, where there was an improvement from poor to poor/moderate.

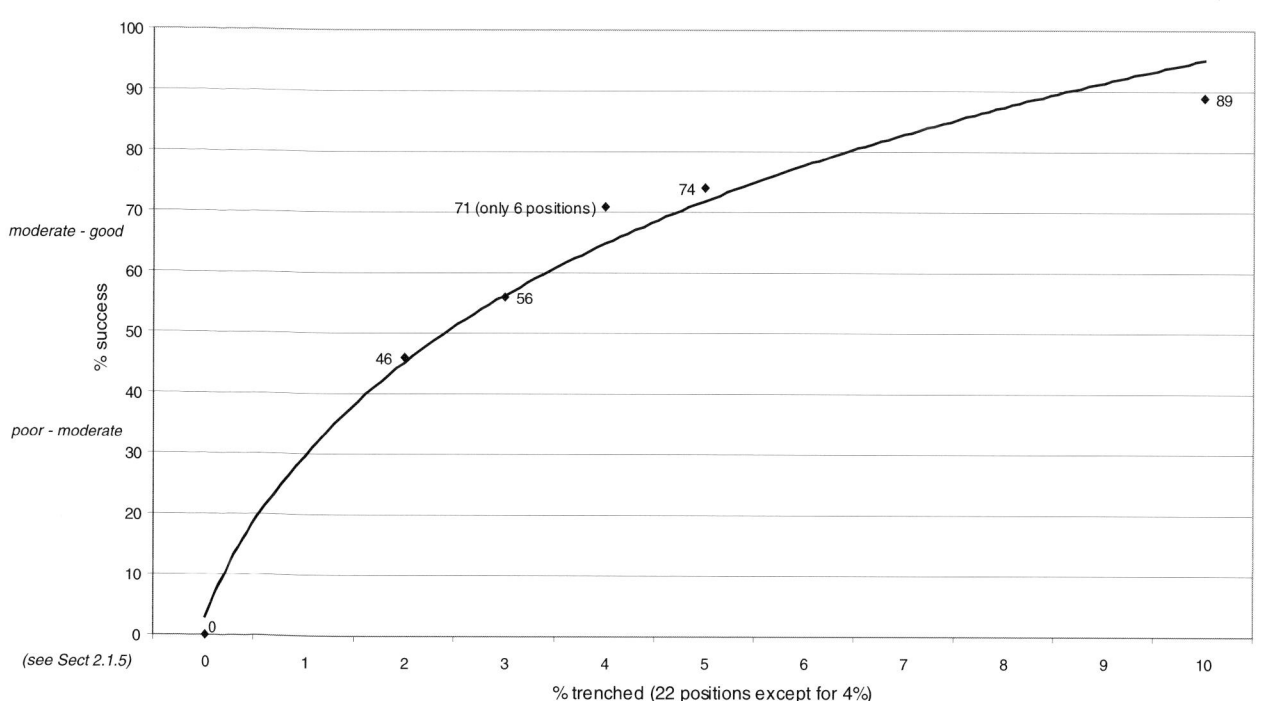

Figure 27 Improvement of success as sample size increases: grid and parallel trenching

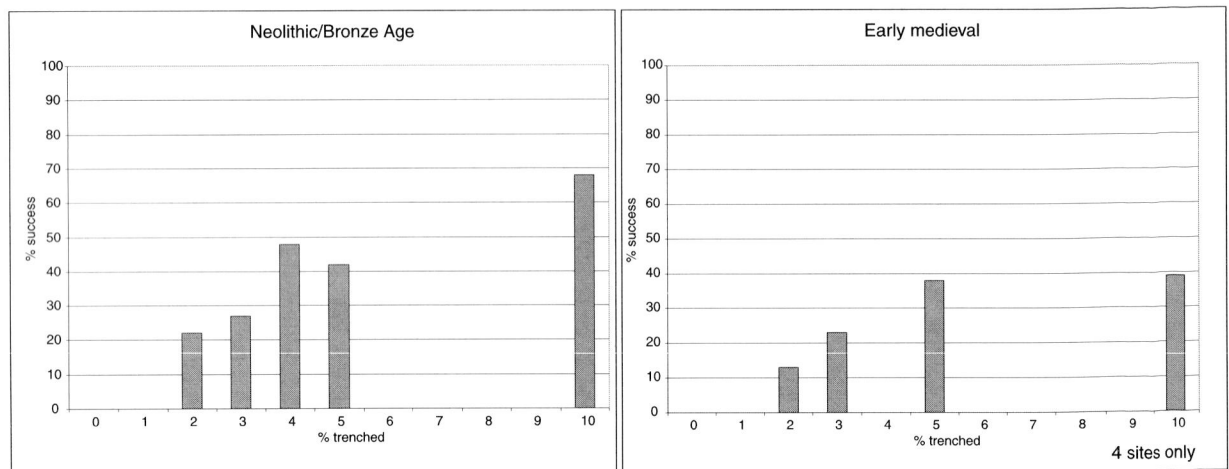

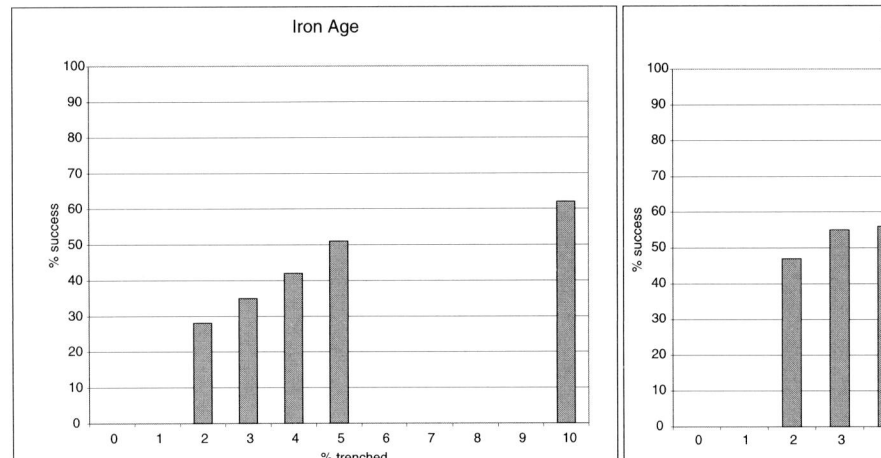

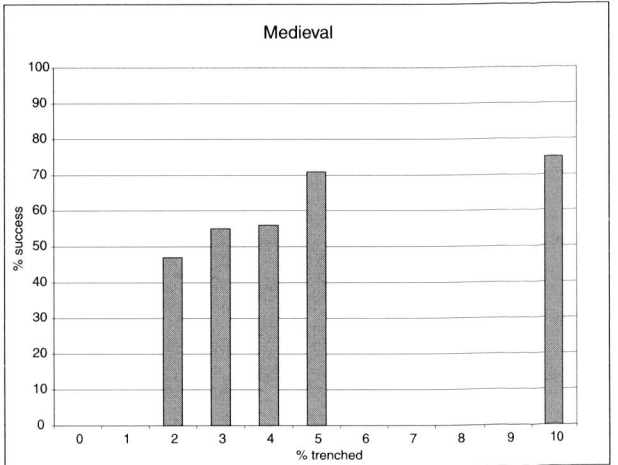

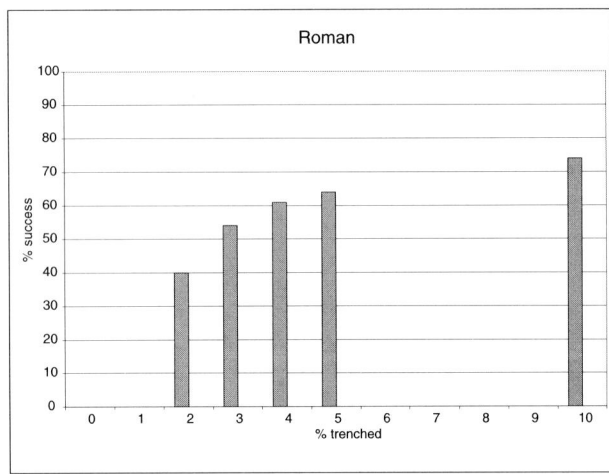

Figure 28 Improvement in success rate as sample size increases for different periods

4.3 Assessing variability

It was apparent from these results, however, that the success of any given trenching array on a particular site could be quite variable, as chance alone can produce a good performance or a bad one. Compare, for example, the greater success of 4% trenching than 5% for evaluating Neolithic and Bronze Age remains on Table 6 and Figure 28. There are numerous other examples in the tables in Appendix 3.

Rather than placing the trenches at random, a series of experiments was set up to assess this variability.

4.3.1 Results of quantification experiments

For seven sites, the archaeological remains that would have been exposed in simulated trenches was quantified and compared to the total area of archaeology found on the excavated area (see above, Section 2.3, for the method and difficulties of achieving this, and Figures 29 and 30 for an illustration of the method). In general it was shown that, as the percentage of the total evaluation area seen increased, the percentage of the total area of archaeology discovered increased accordingly (Table 7). In fact, while the area of archaeology discovered was broadly proportional to the fraction of the entire evaluation area which was trenched, the actual result was usually within a small range on either side of this. In practice this variation was usually within 1% of the expected result, and virtually always within 1.5%. Thus, a strategy of trenching 5% of an evaluation area would be expected to detect approximately 5% of the archaeology within the area; within these simulations it tended to range between 4% and 6% of the archaeology present. The average of these scores was usually slightly below the expected proportion of the archaeology on the site, but there were probably too few examples to create a stable statistical model (see Appendix 3).

Table 7 Results of quantification calculations, showing archaeology discovered (as a percentage by area of total archaeology found)

Array	Sample fraction of array	Thurnham	White Horse Stone	Westhawk Farm Farm	Thanet Way	Tesco Manston Road	Stansted	Yarnton	Average
Grid	2%	2.3	2.1	1.4	3	0.8	1.7	1.7	1.86
Grid	3%	4.3	3.5	2.7	3.8	3.7	2.9	5.5	3.77
Grid	4%	3.2	4.5						3.85
Grid	5%	4.6	3.4	4.1	4.9	6.1	4.8	4.9	4.69
Grid	10%	11.4	9.2	9.1	10.1	11.3	8.8	10	9.99

However, these experiments demonstrated how significant 'chance' can be. On Yarnton Site 7, a 3% array was unusually 'lucky' and succeeded in locating over 5.5% of the archaeology present in the evaluation area, whereas the same array at 5% revealed just under 5% of the archaeology by area. In this case, the simulation with less trenches actually detected more of the archaeology.

It is important to stress that the degree of variability has a much greater impact upon decision-making when the trenching is at low percentages. For example, an experiment based on the Tesco, Manston Road, Ramsgate site resulted in the discovery of only 0.8% of the archaeology by area, despite the use of a 2% trenching strategy (Table 7). As 2% is probably the most common trenching regime requested in this country, the implications of these conclusions are far-reaching.

4.3.2 Best- and worst-case trenches

Simulations on the Thurnham Villa site to examine the best and worst results achievable by an individual array for Arrays 1, 2, 4 and 5 (Table 5), also revealed the unpredictable nature of archaeological evaluations. When considering all periods of archaeology, it was revealed that the performance of an individual trench array could vary greatly (Table 8).

The original random simulation of standard grid trenches at the 3% level produced

Figure 29 Westhawk Farm with 3% trenching

a score of 8 points out of a possible 15 (a poor to moderate result). The experiments showed that the worst possible outcome of this trenching strategy resulted in a score of only 2 points, whereas the best outcome received a score of 12. Each of these two extremes would be unlikely to occur, but they reflect the potential risk involved in the specific evaluation strategy tested. Once again, the smaller the proportion of the area trenched the greater the potential impact of this variability.

In this exercise, in order to guarantee at least a moderate to good result, a sample fraction of greater than 5% would be needed. As no fractions between 5% and 10% were simulated, a precise level cannot be deduced. However, in all the experiments the arrays at 5% did not succeed in achieving a moderate to good result in their

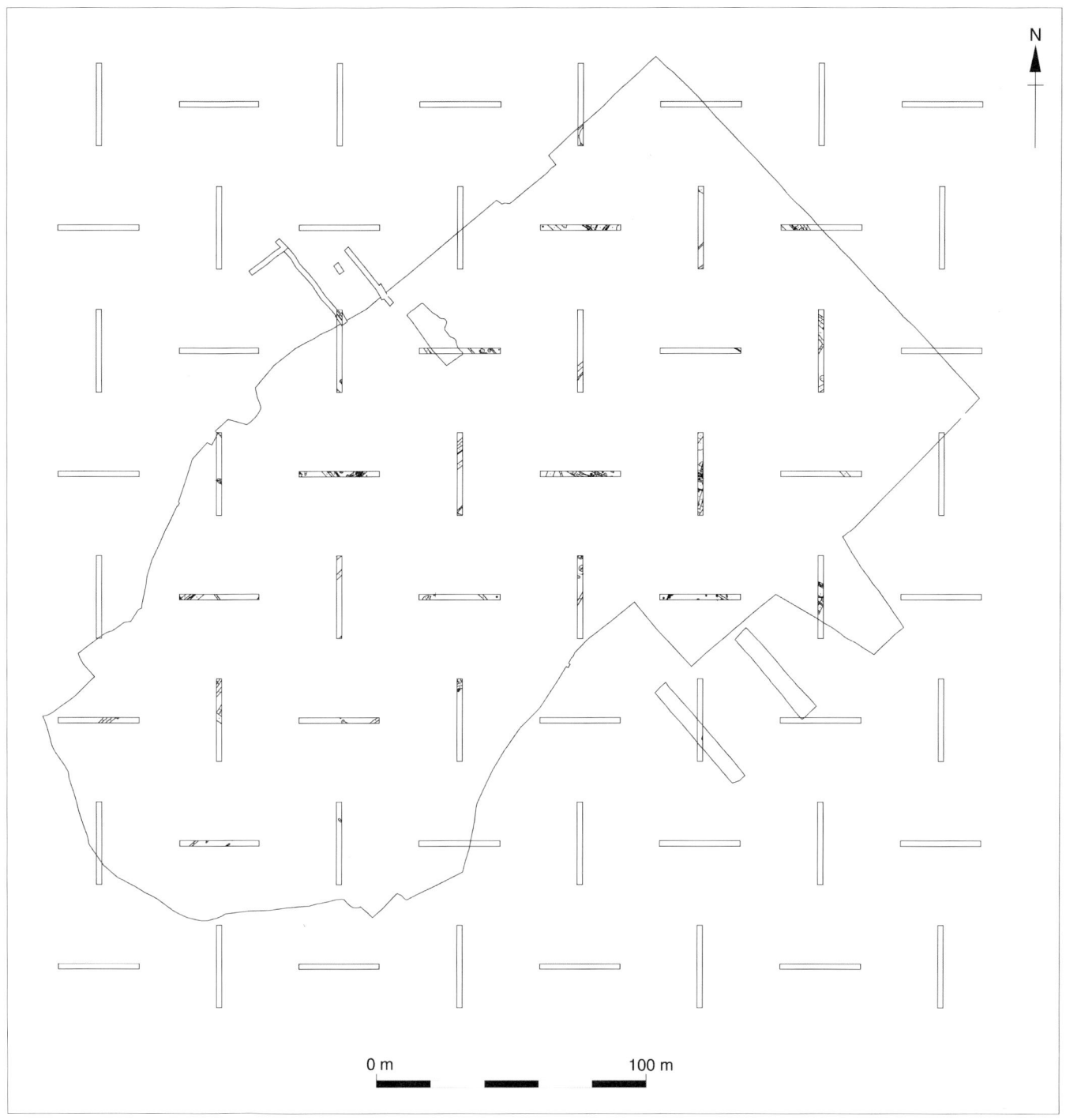

N

Figure 30 Westhawk Farm: archaeological features exposed in 3% trenches

worst case, whereas those at 10% did. It should be stressed that all the above simulations were carried out for the Thurnham Villa site, and that findings are likely to vary according to the different natures of individual sites.

4.3.3   Regular movement of trenches

Two sites with different characteristics were selected to observe the effect of moving a single array (standard grid at 5%) a regular distance of 10 m in each direction, achieving 12 different positions on each site, systematically sampling the site (Table 9). Northumberland Bottom had a range of archaeology of different periods from the Bronze Age to the medieval period and had a number of ditched enclosures and linear features. White Horse Stone, on the other hand, mainly comprised posthole structures in settlements of Neolithic and Iron Age date which were unenclosed. Across the 12 simulations for White Horse Stone (for

Table 8 The results of best- and worst-trench positions

Assessment of best and worst cases (Thurnham Villa)   Score out of a maximum of 15 points

Array	Sample fraction of array	Random Position	Best Outcome	Worst Outcome
1. Standard Grid	2%	4	6	1
	3%	8	12	2
	4%	7	12	4
	5%	10	12	8
2. 20m trenches	2%	3	7	0
	3%	7	10	3
	4%	9	11	7
	5%	10	11	8
4, Aligned (offset)	3%	9	11	1
	5%	10	11	9
	10%	14	15	12
5. Continuous	3%	2	7	4
	5%	11	14	5
	10%	13	15	11

archaeology of all periods) the scores achieved ranged from 8 to 15 (out of a maximum of 15), with an average of 12.4. However, for the Northumberland Bottom site the variation was much less, with the same array producing results between 12 and 14 points, the average being 13.2. A sequential sampling test which randomised the scores and averaged them in sequence, suggests that the average result is stable (see Appendix 3). This shows that the potential and likely variability of the results of an evaluation trenching exercise is, to a certain extent, dependent on the nature of the site itself, many aspects of which would be unknown at the evaluation stage.

When each individual period of archaeology was considered a slightly different picture emerged. Out of the 12 simulations carried out for the Northumberland Bottom site, eight positions achieved a moderate to good or good result for each period of archaeology present, whereas this was achieved by only two White Horse Stone simulations. At Northumberland Bottom, it was the Neolithic/Bronze Age periods alone which were not detected at a moderate to good level on a third of the positions. At White Horse Stone not only did a third of simulated positions fail to detect remains of this period, but simulations also failed to achieve a moderate to good result for the Iron Age period in half of the simulations, and for medieval archaeology in a quarter of cases. These results demonstrate that, not only does the success of the same evaluation technique vary according to the character of the site in question but, even on the same site, its success will differ for each period present.

4.4   Summary of results

The simulations showed that three trench arrays seemed to be similarly effective in most circumstances, the standard grid array with 30 m trenches (Array 1), the grid array with 20 m trenches (Array 2) and the parallel array (Array 4), of which the first produced the more consistent results. Other trench types performed reasonably in certain circumstances, but none of these offered comparable results in all situations. For example, although the array based on continuous trenches (Array 5) was slightly more effective at detecting Bronze Age and Neolithic remains than the standard grid array, in all other circumstances it performed poorly. The full range of periods present on a site is usually uncertain; selecting a method based on its perceived success at

Table 9 Results of moving trenches a regular distance

Variability of results for the Grid array at 5%
Scores out of a maximum of 15 points

Position	White Horse Stone	Northumberland Bottom
1	11	12
2	13	14
3	11	14
4	12	13
5	14	14
6	13	14
7	8	12
8	15	13
9	13	14
10	13	12
11	11	14
12	15	12
Average score	12.4	13.2

detecting features of certain periods may reinforce existing preconceptions concerning the archaeology present. Experiments that looked at the best- and worst-case results of the various arrays under different circumstances also suggested that it would be unwise to adopt the continuous trenching strategy because of the high level of potential variability in the performance of this technique. The grid array with wide trenches (Array 3) was similarly disappointing unless undertaken at high percentages. The first grid array provided a lower risk evaluation strategy, and none of the other trenching arrays produced a significantly better performance in this respect.

In terms of selecting the appropriate sample fraction to use for a trenching array, the simulations revealed that an array at 5% did not guarantee a moderate to good result, although this was usually achieved. However, even the poorest performances at 10% still produced a moderate to good result when archaeology of all periods was considered, so it would appear that the minimum sample fraction still capable of producing this standard of result (even in the worst cases) lies somewhere between these two values. It was also shown that the variability between the best and worst performances of a given array cannot be accurately predicted in advance, because simulations showed that this was partly dependent upon the nature of the site itself.

The issue is complicated by the fact that archaeological remains of different periods benefited to varying degrees from increasing the sample fraction of a trenching array. For example, while using a high sample fraction may be particularly useful when a site contains prehistoric archaeology, for medieval or Roman remains the potential gain may be negligible compared to the increased cost. This once again raises the problem inherent in deciding upon an evaluation trenching strategy on the basis of what archaeological remains are expected.

4.5   Independently evaluating simulations

An archaeologist who was not otherwise involved in this project, or any of those within the study, and who was unaware of the conclusions being drawn from the modelling, examined the results of simulated trenching for some projects, as described above (Section 2.3). He concluded that the success of any sampling strategy rests on the relationship between the sample design (size and frequency of interventions), the type of deposits being evaluated (linear or isolated cuts, or stratified deposits) and the skill/experience of the evaluator.

4.5.1 Types of deposit

This experiment examined the effectiveness of the standard grid array at a range of sample size (as, for example, on Fig. 30), with each size being observed independently, in sequence and in order of magnitude. The study showed that at 2%, sites containing linear features such as enclosed Iron Age or Roman settlements were nearly always located (if not adequately characterised). Sites comprising predominantly isolated features, such as earlier prehistoric or Saxon settlements were much less predictable. They could be detected as one or two features at 2%, but then not be detected at 3% or even 5%, only reappearing at 10%. Even Romano-British sites without strong linear components were often difficult to identify. As with the other simulations, this experiment showed the extent to which much depended on luck in trench location; 3% trenching may entirely miss a group of Bronze Age pits in one particular position, but hit them if laid out in another way. Only the 10% sample appeared to be a fully reliable design in terms of identifying isolated features every time.

4.5.2 Sample design

Plans of the archaeological features revealed in trenching at 2% showed that it was often possible to identify the basic archaeological components within a study area, particularly the major periods of occupation and the main foci of activity (although small concentrations of isolated features were often missed as explained above). It was usually possible to form an opinion of the significance of the deposits and the recommended mitigation strategy, neither of which changed fundamentally with more data gained from more detailed evaluations. However, this did involve an amount of courage and risk. At 2%, judgements may be based on the occurrence of a single Saxon pit, for example. It would be necessary to err on the generous side in designing any mitigation from such a level of work; in most cases the recommendation might be a full topsoil-strip of the majority of the study area. In the real world such decisions might be difficult to defend and could cause severe problems if a greater than predicted level of archaeology was subsequently discovered (or embarrassment if significantly less was found). On the single linear project considered, a 2% sample was wholly inadequate, possibly because the overall linear shape of the study area had already introduced a bias into the identification of what were non-linear sites.

At 3% it was possible to refine the picture but a significant gain was often made at 5% where the detail of a site's character was often revealed, or previously invisible types of deposits or periods of activity detected. At 10% the data was subject to diminishing returns. Much of what had already been known about the site was being duplicated, the same ditch being picked up between points already established for instance, or more pits within a general area of pitting being exposed.

4.5.3 Skill/experience of the archaeologist

Probably the key factor in the success of any evaluation is the professional judgement of the archaeologist called upon to interpret the results. The current study was somewhat artificial in this respect, as only the two-dimensional trench plans were available, no site visits nor topographical/historical investigations could be undertaken, and no detailed plans, sections nor context descriptions could be consulted. Background knowledge beyond the specific evidence associated with a site is of great importance, including a knowledge of the local/regional archaeology, the physical conditions of burial and survival and local geologies. For example, the person undertaking this experiment struggled when faced with buried sarsen stones, yet felt quite comfortable with boulder clay; having excavated a small Romano-British shrine allowed him to instantly recognise the fragment of tell-tale gully surrounding an example within an evaluation trench.

4.5.4 Final conclusions

Despite the assertion that a brave and knowledgeable curator might be able to work with a 2% sample, in reality this does not appear to supply the level of confidence required when making planning decisions that might need to be defended at Enquiry. At a sample of between 3% and 5%, enough information was generally available to provide an assessment of the site to meet planning requirements and form the basis for designing a mitigation strategy. At 5% some of the extra trenches picked up features already seen at 2% or 3%, particularly linear ditches but, even so, there were also very often unanswered questions about the site at lower percentages that could have a material impact on its interpretation, and on the decisions made with regard to its preservation and/or excavation. These questions can often be identified in the field and, if a contingency exists, extra trenches may be excavated to address them. It may be appropriate to design evaluations as a two-stage exercise, stage one involving a more or less random trenching at 3% - 4% and stage two a targeted, problem-orientated investigation. This would involve a rapid assessment and feedback of the stage one results in order to identify the questions, if any, for stage two.

5   COST-EFFECTIVENESS

5.1   The cost of evaluation

The cost of archaeological evaluation work undertaken on the projects that formed part of this study is estimated to be in the order of 7% of the total archaeological cost. The most expensive, and among the most commonly used evaluation technique, machine trenching, probably costs around 4% of the total; other methods were cheaper (desk-based assessment 0.5%; fieldwalking 1%; geophysical survey 0.9% and test pits 0.4%).

The range of evaluation techniques employed varied considerably from project to project, and the intensity to which the various methods were used also differed. A per-hectare cost was calculated, therefore, for each evaluation strategy used on each project, by dividing the estimated cost of the technique by the area over which it was used, and the results are expressed as units. The costs of the main techniques are shown in Figure 31 in proportion to each other.

5.1.1   Desk-based assessments

Desk-based assessment was the most frequently used of the evaluation methods, being used on all sites. For these projects, desk-based assessment was the cheapest technique, being only approximately 4% of the total evaluation cost per hectare (8 units) and, in a simple equation which divides the effectiveness of the techniques by the cost of the work, desk-based assessment achieved the highest scores. However, its limitations are well recognised and are demonstrated on Figure 32, where its success on these particular projects was not even poor to moderate, even though some of these assessments were based on detailed previous knowledge. In other words, it would be very difficult on the basis of these desk-based assessments to predict archaeological remains, and very easy to miss sites of significance. As such, it may be cheap but it is not cost-effective as a stand-alone evaluation technique. However, desk-based assessments are not usually employed in this country to reveal this kind of information, but are the first stage at which the broad potential of the area and its physical characteristics are defined before deciding appropriate assessment techniques. As such they are invaluable, and it must be recognised that some important remains found on some of the projects within this study were only predicted at desk-based assessment stage, for example Neolithic remains at White Horse Stone and the Saxon cemetery at Thanet Way, demonstrating the importance of informed judgement. For these reasons, and as long as its limitations are appreciated, desk-based assessment can be considered to be money well spent.

5.1.2   Fieldwalking

Fieldwalking costs more than three times as much as desk-based assessment on these projects per hectare (27 units), although it was still a comparatively cheap technique (Fig. 31). Overall, it was not significantly more successful than desk-based assessment, producing only poor to moderate results. However, the success of fieldwalking on these projects was very variable and it could be very effective in some circumstances, in particular for identifying the presence of Neolithic and Bronze Age sites (see below; Fig. 32). Indeed, as burnt stone spreads not associated with underlying archaeological features at Thurnham Villa and White Horse Stone show, it may be the only method of locating early sites that only survive in the ploughsoil and as such it has particular value. Over the clay soils at Stansted, Essex, the correspondence of fieldwalking finds with underlying remains was particularly good for the later prehistoric period (Fig. 13), and this method of evaluation is strongly advocated in Essex (Medlycott and Germany 1994). Roman sites are often easily recognised by these means (eg Fig. 12). Nevertheless, fieldwalking depends on the presence of durable material remains and, where these are absent, sites will

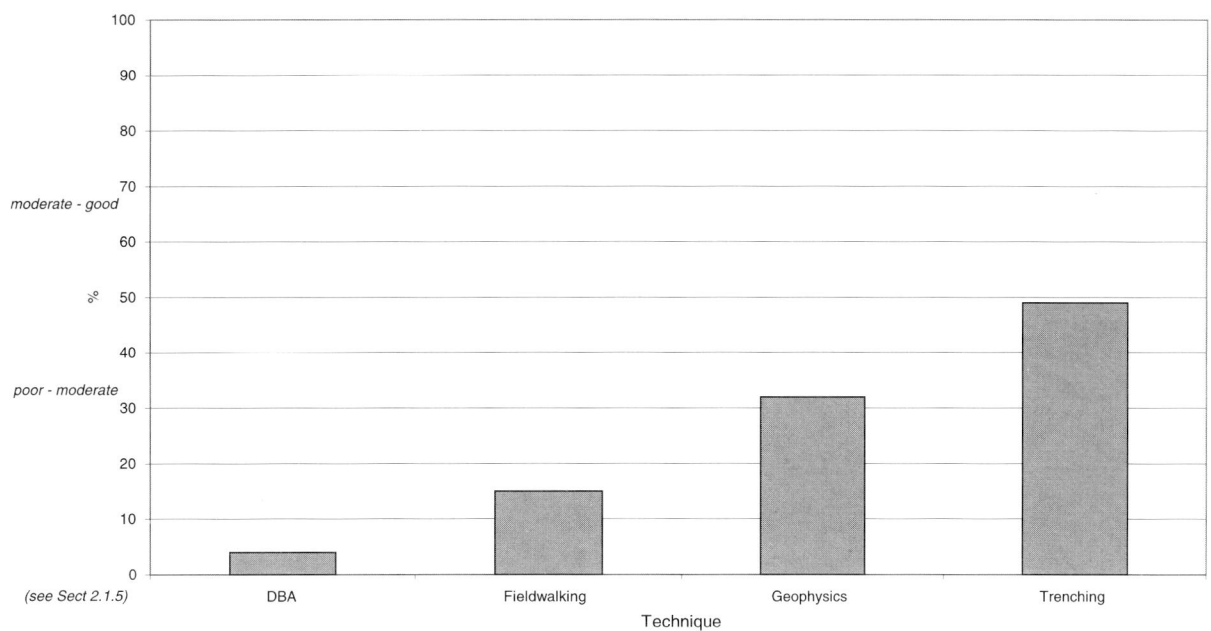

Figure 31 Relative cost of evaluation techniques

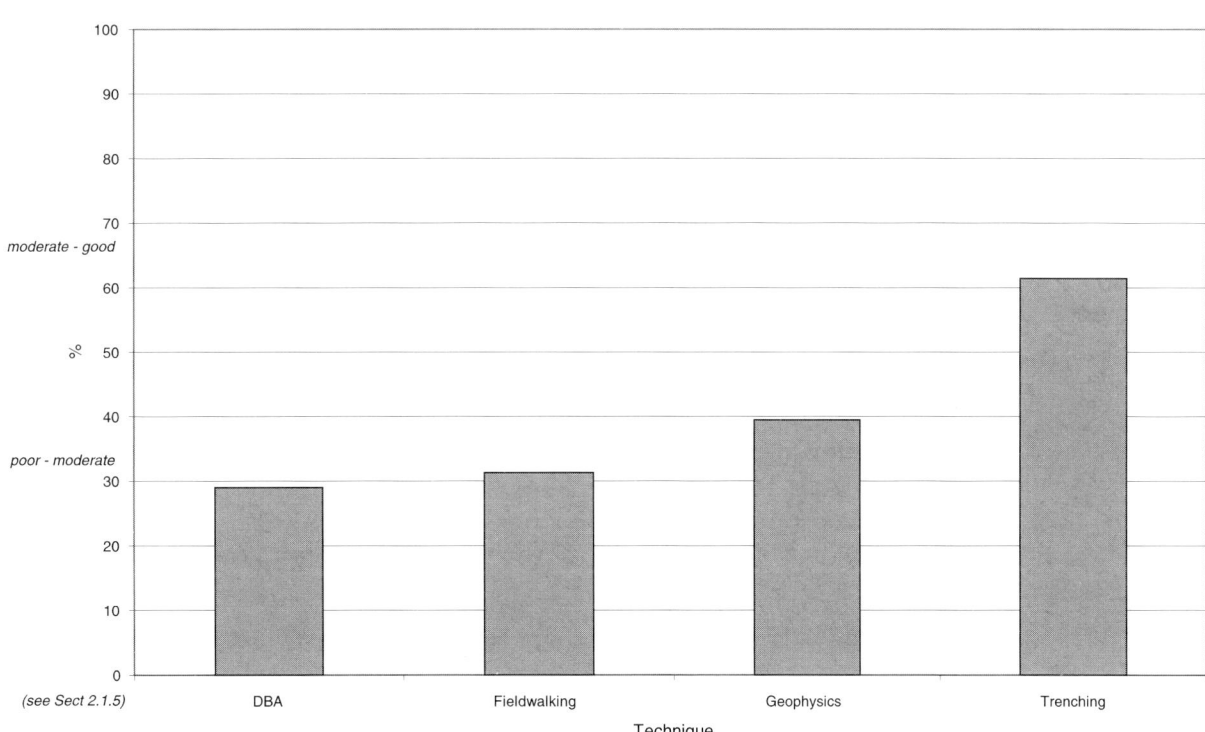

Figure 32 Success of techniques for all periods

be missed. Perhaps for this reason, it was a particularly poor technique for locating the Saxon sites in this study; it seemed to explain the low recovery of Iron Age finds in parts of East Anglia (Pryor *et al.* 1985, 310-1). In addition, it has obvious drawbacks over deeply-buried sites and reveals very little information on the state of preservation and extent of the archaeological remains beneath.

5.1.3. *Geophysical survey*

Geophysical survey is a more expensive technique than any of the other non-intrusive methods (57 units; Fig. 31). It was more effective than these within this particular group of projects, but it must be remembered that it was usually only selected for use in favourable circumstances. It was not employed on some of the sites where colluvial deposits were known to be present, therefore, such as White Horse Stone and Thanet Way. However, its success over the Roman site of Elms Farm, covered by alluvium, may not have been anticipated and demonstrates that for certain types of archaeological remains it is very effective. Roman settlements and Neolithic and Bronze Age funerary monuments were particularly suitable subjects among the sites in this study; ring ditches and a Neolithic long enclosure were visible beneath alluvium on the floodplain at Yarnton, for example (eg Figs 2 and 15). The method can reveal site layout more clearly than other techniques and thus suggest conditions of preservation and site character. On the other hand, dating of features can be achieved only by inference. More importantly, its inability to locate smaller features must be recognised, especially posthole structures, pit alignments and other more ephemeral remains.

5.1.4   *Test pits*

As test pits were not used as a site detection method on any of the projects in this study, their effectiveness cannot be assessed. However, individual pits (1 m x 1 m) dug by hand with soil sieving are not a cheap option, although the price would depend upon the depth and character of the soils. Light, sandy soils may not present so much of a problem but sieving clay soils is a nightmare. We estimate, for these projects, an array of pits spaced every 20 m (in our experience the most common array requested in southern England) would cost more than three times the cost per hectare of machine trenching. The simulation exercise shows how ineffective such a technique can be, as it consistently produced very poor results. Test-pitting can be undertaken by machine, making it a more rapid and thus cheaper method, but its lack of success would still make it very poor value for money. Test pits can have an important place in field evaluation for investigating soil development and post-depositional processes on site, and dating material in the ploughsoil, but they are more cheaply and effectively done in conjunction with machine trenching, when horizons can be clearly seen and soil can be thrown down into an open trench. Their role in excavating ploughsoil finds is well recognised and irreplaceable.

5.1.5   *Machine trenching*

Machine trenching was the most expensive method used on these projects per hectare (87 units), representing approximately half of the total evaluation costs (Fig. 31). It was, however, the only technique to provide moderate to good results in evaluation which would allow reasonable confidence in a decision to proceed to further investigation (Fig. 32). It was the only method to adequately address issues of preservation and the quality of finds. Importantly, it could be used on all of these projects, regardless of whether they had been ploughed or were too deeply buried for non-intrusive methods. In half of the projects within the study, it was the critical factor which led to further investigation, without which further work would have been unlikely (Northumberland Bottom, White Horse Stone, Ramsgate Harbour Approach, Whitfield to Eastry Bypass, Tesco Manston Road and Yarnton). However, as we have seen, its success varied greatly according to the period of the remains and character of the site, the intensity and design of the trenching regime and also depended, to some degree, on chance in the positioning of trenches.

5.1.6   *Confidence versus cost*

The simulation exercises showed that moderate to good results could be achieved when between 3% and 4% of the site was evaluated by trenching (using data from the standard grid array and parallel trench array that was simulated on eleven of the sites; Fig. 23). This would seem to represent good value. However, to **guarantee** this degree of confidence between 5% and 10% of the site should be seen (see above Section 4.3). This places the curator in a dilemma because the increase in knowledge gained is not proportional to the increase in effort, as shown in Figure 27. Also the costs rise inexorably, even though there is a small saving of scale to be

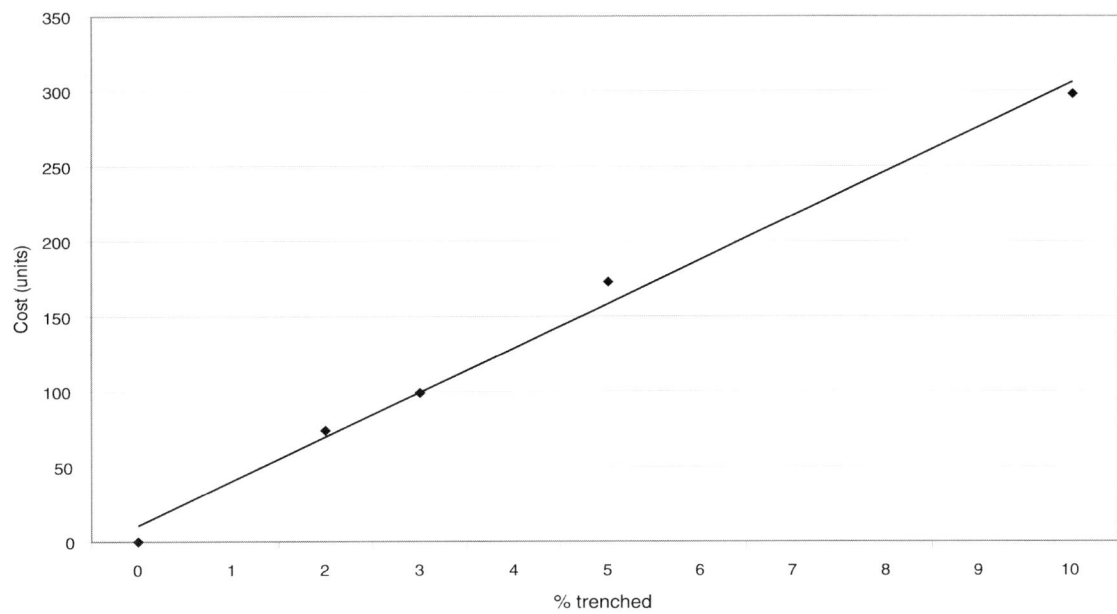

Figure 33 Increase in cost in relation to increased trenching

made when trenching more intensively (Fig. 33; compare with Fig. 27). What is cost effective and what can be considered reasonable to request a developer to fund in these circumstances?

There is an additional problem. Evaluating Roman and medieval remains is comparatively straightforward, as indicated above, and some measure of confidence in the results can be achieved at moderate sampling levels (Fig. 28). These are also the periods for which there is least to gain from increasing the size of the evaluation to high levels. But, as we have seen, this is not true of all periods. There was a greater increase of knowledge between 5% and 10% for Neolithic and Bronze Age sites in this study, and some important features were not detected even in a 10% sample strategy (eg Fig. 22). Saxon settlements appear to be even harder to locate (Fig. 28). Chance plays a much more significant part in the discovery of these remains and no evaluation technique seems to represent very good value for money. Given the significance of this kind of archaeology and its rarity in the archaeological record, is it more prudent and cost-effective to move straight to stripping entire sites, and planning and rapidly examining the remains (strip, map and sample; see below), rather than evaluating in advance? It is, after all, in the extensive excavation areas opened on these projects to examine the remains of other periods that some of the most significant (and unexpected) discoveries came to light.

5.2   Strip, map and sample

The strip, map and sample approach needs to be considered from a variety of viewpoints. In the first place, it must be recognised that some of the most important gains in archaeological knowledge in recent years have come as a result of stripping large areas where it has been possible to look at settlement dynamics and the explicit relationship between groups of features within their wider cultural and natural environment, rather than focusing on concentrations of activity and surmising (or ignoring) the character of the spaces between. More ephemeral remains have emerged unexpectedly in these situations, and these can make a significant contribution to the understanding of the past, the Neolithic long houses at White Horse Stone and Yarnton being obvious examples. The strip, map and sample method assumes that the archaeology uncovered will be sampled rather than fully excavated, the settlement plan being paramount. Sampling can be used to characterise the various elements of a site, to establish a chronological framework and to investigate in more depth significant foci of activity, but not necessarily to excavate all the archaeology fully. Its advantage is that sampling decisions can be taken in terms of the totality of the archaeology as seen in plan at an early stage, rather than just a small proportion. On rural sites with comparatively dispersed remains and 'horizontal' stratigraphy, the character of many of the sites within this study, this method merits serious consideration (see below), although there are situations in which strip, map and sample is not appropriate, for example complex, deeply stratified sites.

It has been difficult to undertake detailed comparative costings of strip map and sample as against evaluation and excavation, because of differences in objectives and philosophical approaches to the archaeology which cannot be divorced from costing issues, as discussed above (Section 2.4). This was compounded by the varied character of these projects, the density and complexity of remains, practical differences in the way they would be stripped, and the degree of extra work that might be required in order to investigate adequately major components of them. Roman villas and towns are obvious examples of sites where additional work, and therefore money, would be needed, but extra funding would also have been required for some of the more complicated settlement and burial features. It was not easy to estimate the amount that would need to be set aside for this work.

The estimated costs suggested that stripping, mapping and sampling sites, followed by additional work, would usually have been cheaper than the estimated cost of all archaeological investigations that were undertaken. The savings per hectare appeared to be greatest where more intense evaluation was carried out (for example Ramsgate Harbour Approach Road and Tesco Manston Road), or where a suite of techniques was employed (as at Elms Farm or Yarnton). Sites with more dispersed remains also appeared to be more cost-effectively examined in this fashion (eg Whitfield to Eastry Bypass and parts of Yarnton), but for more densely-occupied sites with more complex stratigraphy this would not necessarily be the case.

The Thanet Way and Stansted projects adopted an approach that most closely resembled the strip-map-and-sample method (see above, Section 3.3.8), and the estimates suggested that the total of the per-hectare costs of each evaluation technique and the excavations conducted on these projects were cheaper than the majority of other sites. However, it must be stressed that the cost of the excavations was largely a reflection of the period and complexity of the remains. On both these projects the character of the development was such that stripping for archaeological purposes could be undertaken within the construction processes, with main phase of archaeological excavation following the sample evaluation of features immediately.

There are ramifications in the planning process for the use of the strip-map-and-sample strategy, the most significant of which is the inability, or increased difficulty, of discussing preservation of remains *in situ*, or effecting alterations to development designs. In addition, it would be important to consider:

- how to allocate appropriate funds to the project
- how to assess its likely duration and avert major delays to development which are for some schemes the most critical and costly factor
- how to argue in the planning process that archaeological conditions are reasonable practical problems for developers when stripped areas are exposed to degradation for a longer period
- how to operate a tendering process for the work which enables archaeological contractors to bid for work on an equal footing, and where quality and efficiency can be taken into account in addition to a cheap price

Whatever the circumstances of particular projects, there remains a central issue, which is that our standard evaluation techniques are not discovering some of our most exciting archaeological remains, and are reinforcing biases current in the archaeological record. Are we prepared to miss more ephemeral features, or consign their discovery to chance? For the projects that formed part of this study, evaluation was not an expensive part of the archaeological process (c 7%), although the intensity of these assessments was not as great as might be desirable (Table 3). The most expensive, and time-consuming, archaeology to excavate, and hence the greatest impediment to a strip-map-and-sample solution, is that of the Romano-British and medieval periods which has not been anticipated. These are also the sites which are easiest to evaluate cost-effectively. Judiciously selecting techniques to locate such deposits, followed by stripping, mapping and sampling with a contingency available for more ephemeral remains, may be the way forward.

6 CONCLUSIONS

This pilot study has examined projects which uncovered significant archaeological remains. Some of the discoveries were unexpected at the early planning stages and, in some cases, even when the sites were stripped for excavation. They provide an excellent resource for examining the issues of archaeological decision-making processes and sampling strategies. They show how difficult it can be to evaluate archaeological sites and suggest that we may be systematically missing some aspects of the past which are difficult to detect.

6.1. Evaluation methods in relation to physical circumstances

The project was a pilot study and only a limited number of sites were examined; furthermore their physical attributes were somewhat diverse. Consequently, a definitive assessment of the appropriateness of different techniques in different conditions was not possible, but important questions worthy of examination in greater depth were raised. On the whole, larger sites were easier to evaluate than those covering a small area, and linear schemes slightly more problematic than those which encompassed a broader area. The impact of geology, the depth and character of overburden and the nature of recent land use seemed to have less of an impact on the success of evaluation than the date and character of the archaeological remains.

6.2 Non-intrusive evaluation methods

Comparing the different techniques has shown that all methods have advantages and disadvantages.

Desk-based assessment is not usually a sufficiently thorough method of evaluation to enable a confident judgement to be made about the presence of archaeological remains, unless detailed evidence about adjacent areas is available. It is, however, a very cost-effective way of enabling appropriate strategies for further work to be considered, and proved excellent value on the projects in this study.

The success of fieldwalking depends on the presence of cultivated land and proximity of archaeological remains to the modern surface (usually, but see Hey 1998). It also relies on the presence of durable artefacts associated with the site, a circumstance that does not always apply. It was, however, the only technique of evaluation used at Stansted Long-term Car Park, where it provided a very good guide to underlying features (eg Fig. 13). For discovering Saxon sites its effectiveness was poor. Geophysical survey also was dependent upon suitable physical circumstances, and relied more on the presence of reasonably substantial and responsive archaeological remains. Thus it was fairly successful at finding Roman settlements and Bronze Age ring ditches, but poor at finding posthole structures of any period. Where it was effective, it could provide an excellent preview of a site from which to develop excavation strategies, but where less substantial remains survived it could be misleading, suggesting that archaeological remains were absent. On balance, non-intrusive methods can provide very good value for money if they are chosen judiciously, and their limitations are appreciated.

6.3 Intrusive methods of evaluation and the results of computer simulations

Of the intrusive methods, only machine trenching was assessed in any detail within this project. It was the most expensive evaluation method, but it was the only technique of any type to provide moderate to good results, and the only adequate method of locating scattered remains. The state of preservation of the physical remains and the date of surviving features were only effectively assessed by trenching.

Simulations of trenching on the projects in this study (described in Section 4) showed that, on the whole, three arrays performed similarly: a standard grid array with 30 m x 2 m trenches; a grid array with 20 m x 2 m trenches; and a parallel array with lines offset from each other (Fig. 20). Two other arrays, a grid array with wide trenches and continuous trenches produced comparable results at higher percentages (ie 10%), but were significantly less effective when only 2% and 3% was sampled. Centre-line trenching (which is variable in terms of the proportion of the area seen according to the size of the project) and the 'Ramsgate Harbour array' produced only moderate results. The results of test pitting (1 m x 1 m) at 20 m intervals were very poor. On the whole, therefore, trenching arrays commonly used in this country were similarly effective on these sites, but those techniques resulting in wide gaps between sampling units performed poorly at low densities.

Overall scores mask considerable variation between periods for, as discussed above, Roman and medieval remains were much easier to locate than those of Neolithic, Bronze Age and early medieval/Anglo-Saxon date. Results for individual sites also could be very variable. In an experiment to assess the impact of chance in the trenching process, the total amount of archaeology present on the excavated sites was calculated, and compared with the amounts exposed in simulated evaluation trenches. Did trenching at 5%, for example, really find 5% of the archaeological remains? This work revealed that variation within the sample fraction was usually within ± 1% of the expected results, and nearly always within 1.5%. This has important implications at low sampling fractions; at one site within this study 2% trenching, currently the most commonly-requested sampling strategy in England, found only 0.8% of the archaeology.

Experiments to assess the best and worst-case trench positions and the effect of moving trenches a regular distance to achieve 12 positions for each array suggested that even a 5% sample did not **guarantee** a moderate to good result, whereas 10% did. But the results also showed that variability is to a certain extent dependent upon the nature of the site itself, many aspects of which would be unknown at the evaluation stage.

6.4 Evaluation in relation to different periods and types of archaeological remains

This study demonstrated that the most important variable in the evaluation process was the date, and character of the buried deposits. A breakdown by period shows that for the Neolithic and Bronze Age periods, no technique used on these projects yielded even moderate results (Fig. 34), although the simulations indicate that dense trenching regimes (of between 6% and 10%) may be more successful (Fig. 28). Fieldwalking had some merit, especially in locating sites and, particularly, in establishing the presence of sites that had been entirely disarticulated by the plough. Geophysical survey was successful in locating monuments but not the more ephemeral remains that are the major component of archaeological sites of these periods. The success of this method for the Neolithic and Bronze Age would be considerably reduced if funerary monuments and other ditched enclosures were discounted. It is interesting that half the sites in this study produced important remains of these periods only at the stripping stage.

The Iron Age sites found on these projects were most effectively evaluated by machine trenching, which produced moderate to good results (Fig. 35). Geophysical survey could be effective, for example in locating pits and house gullies on responsive geologies (eg on gravel terrace at Yarnton), but where remains were more ephemeral,

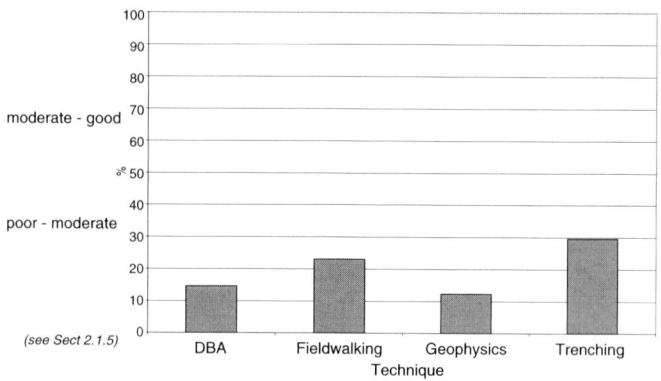

Figure 34 Success of techniques for Neolithic/Bronze Age period

(see Sect 2.1.5)

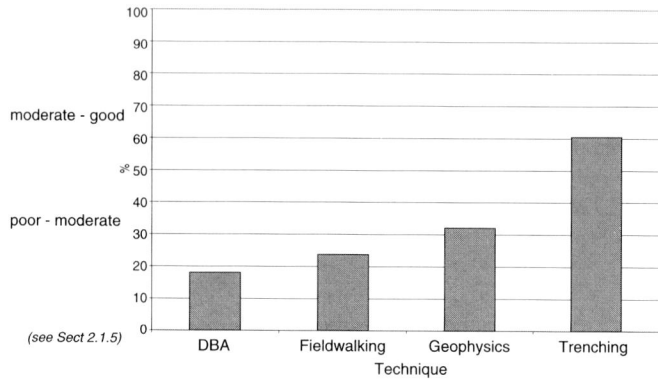

Figure 35 Success of techniques for Iron Age period

(see Sect 2.1.5)

or were masked by the more magnetic remains of later periods they were difficult to locate by these means.

All evaluation methods produced their best results on Roman sites (Fig. 36). However, even over remains of this period, fieldwalking and geophysics were only moderately successful at best. This was largely because of their inability to assess the state of preservation and quality of the surviving remains. Metal detecting also had some success over this kind of site. Machine trenching, however, produced good results on these projects and represented good value for money.

Saxon remains were the most difficult to evaluate within the projects in this study (Fig. 37). It should be stressed that sites of this period were only found on five projects, but experience elsewhere supports this conclusion (*cf* Lewis *et al.* 1997, 86). No method was even moderately good at detecting these sites, although sunken-featured buildings were detected by magnetometer survey at Yarnton, and one lucky evaluation trench at Tesco Manston Road found the end of a sunken-featured building. Fieldwalking was especially poor.

Medieval remains were nearly as easy to find as those of the Roman period, although fieldwalking was not as effective a technique here (Fig. 38). Machine trenching was the most successful method, and was most effective where there were ditched boundaries and other linear features.

In essence, the extent to which a site comprises ditched enclosures and boundaries as opposed to posthole structures, nucleated as opposed to scattered remains and magnetically-enhanced soils and finds-rich deposits is crucial to the ease with which it can be detected.

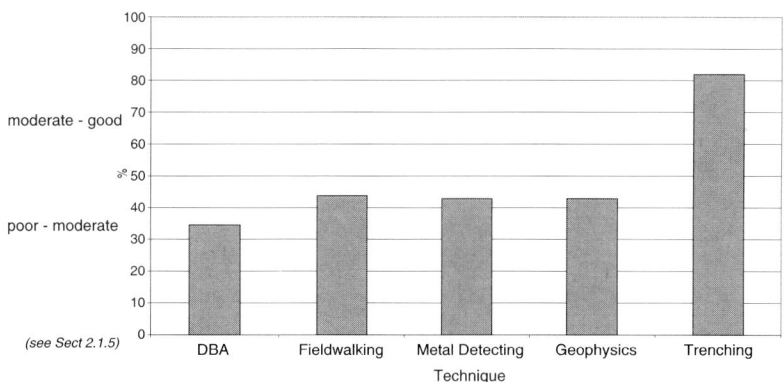

Figure 36 Success of techniques for Roman period

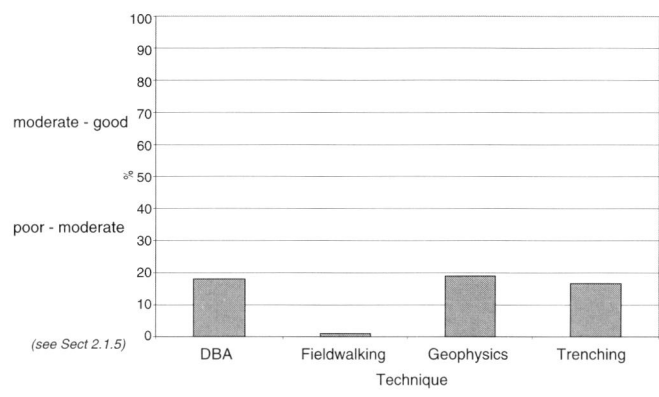

Figure 37 Success of techniques for early medieval (Anglo-Saxon) period

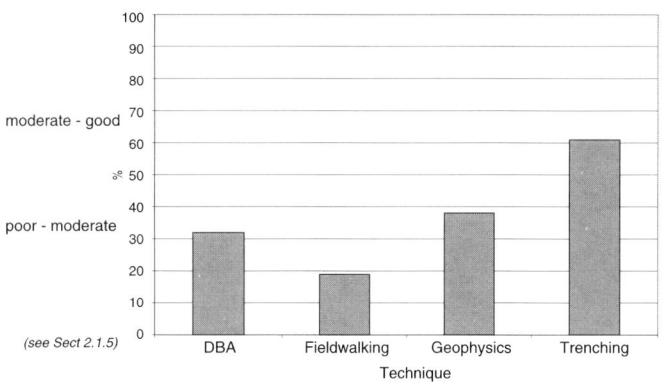

Figure 38 Success of techniques for medieval period

6.5   Implications for the decision-making process

Every project has its own particular combination of circumstances, and there can be no blanket solution to the problems of evaluating all archaeological sites, but it is to be hoped that this study has provided food for thought. Some key issues have been raised and interesting results have emerged. Thus some techniques performed well in certain circumstances, for example fieldwalking for finding Neolithic and Bronze Age sites and geophysics for some Anglo-Saxon settlement features, such as sunken-featured buildings in some circumstances, but these remains still prove elusive. Finding Roman, Iron Age and medieval sites poses less of a challenge, but ephemeral elements even of these periods can be problematical.

A combination of techniques can prove very efficient. The use of small-scale trenching to supplement geophysical survey made the Westhawk Farm evaluation very cost effective, for example.   Similarly, adopting a multi-phase approach to evaluation allows a more problem-orientated investigation and strengthens the interpretation of the results.

Computer simulations of alternative strategies on the sites within the study provided particularly thought-provoking results. These suggest that trench-evaluation strategies in this country are commonly undertaken at too-low densities to evaluate adequately archaeological remains. The potential variability resulting from chance positioning of trenches (of up to 1.5%) makes evaluation of 2% of an area a high-risk strategy. However, increasing the density of trenching does not necessarily result in a proportional improvement in information. The curve of information gained for the simulations undertaken here suggests that, in general, trenching above the 4% to 5% level may not provide good value for money for Romano-British and medieval sites, although for earlier periods this is not the case (Fig. 28).

The study highlights the difficulties of locating precisely the kind of archaeology that is providing new and exciting results for British archaeology, and suggests that a much more problem-orientated approach to evaluation should be adopted.

There are situations in which the area or corridor of development is immovable or constrained, and/or mitigation by a design alteration is not an option. In such cases, there are strong grounds for advocating a strip, map and sample strategy. Forward planning could enable sufficient time to sample remains and allow more-detailed recording of some. Infrastructure projects such as roads and railways are obvious cases where routes may be fixed and where extensive stripping would take place during construction. Moving quickly to strip, map and sample may also be appropriate where rapid, non-intrusive evaluation methods (such as desk-based assessment and fieldwalking) suggest few impediments to development, but suggest that ephemeral remains may be present. Strip, map and sample can provide best value for money on sites too where there is, for some reason, a fixed and tight budget for archaeology, as it can ensure that money is targeted at the most significant remains.

Currently, a high proportion of evaluations in this country are conducted before the outcome of a planning application is decided. In this case strip, map and sample may be unsuitable, and the curator will fall back on more traditional methods of evaluation and excavation. It is hoped that this study has highlighted the advantages and disadvantages of different strategies that could be adopted. Combining different evaluation methods may be appropriate and the use of a two-stage sampling process, or a contingency allowance of trenches, may enable evaluations to be more problem-orientated and hence effective. An awareness of the kinds of archaeological remains that can be missed by all evaluation techniques will enable the adoption of a more effective mitigation strategy, but there will remain a problem of predicting the unusual.

There may be solutions to this dilemma, however. The most expensive and time-consuming excavations are those for which evaluation is comparatively successful. Conscientious evaluation should locate most Roman, Iron Age and medieval remains, even at moderate percentages (Fig. 28). The kind of archaeology that will not be located by these means is also that which can be examined often comparatively quickly and without great expense. Contingencies of time and money built into a development programme would enable most of these to be investigated adequately as they were revealed during stripping. The problems of evaluating such sites should be acknowledged openly; it is not possible to find everything in evaluation. There is good reason to be more daring about suggesting large-scale stripping having first assessed the risk of expensive archaeology in a cost-effective fashion.

We are living in exciting times. Current archaeological excavations are revealing evidence of the past on a scale not previously imagined. These include the dispersed remains of Neolithic and Bronze Age settlements, waterholes, burnt stone deposits and burials made away from funerary monuments which are challenging our preconceptions of Neolithic and Bronze Age settlement in England. Saxon settlements are emerging in areas where previously they were scarce, and small unmarked Anglo-Saxon cemeteries are being found, including Christian burials made before the use of parish graveyards. Knowledge is increasing about Roman and medieval landscape and land use. Settlement is found on geologies which were not thought to be suitable for occupation in the past; the clay lands and the floodplains. These results are emerging because curators and heritage managers feel justified in requesting large-scale excavation in advance of development.

6.6   The way forward

This study had focused on twelve major infrastructure projects in the south-east of England. They provided extensive excavation and watching-brief areas on which to assess the range of techniques used in their evaluation, and on which to simulate alternative strategies. Their physical attributes, in terms of topography, geology and depth of overlying soils were too variable to assess reliably the impact of these factors upon the success of the evaluation techniques. More importantly, circumstances such as depth of overburden varied considerably over individual projects (Table 2) but time did not permit a detailed investigation of the correlation between these specific aspects of the site and the success of different methods of evaluation. Useful information would come from more intensive and problem-orientated analysis of the effect of changing circumstances in just a few cases, perhaps where transects across different geologies and topographical conditions could be achieved.

Although a broad range of sites was investigated, they were typical of projects in south-east England. All sites, with the exception of Elms Farm, had been plough damaged to some extent, with few surviving floors or surfaces. Investigation of a range of sites preserved beneath pasture, and with intact archaeological horizons may provide different results which would be of great value to curators faced with their potential destruction. Similarly, although some of the sites had a considerable depth of colluvium, and to a lesser extent alluvium, over them, none were uniformly deeply buried. Sites in major river valleys and fens, where archaeological remains may lie beneath more than 4 m of overburden have different problems. Some of these issues are addressed by other investigations within this Planarch project (Goudswaard forthcoming; Waugh forthcoming).

It is a feature of the studies that have been undertaken on evaluation strategies to date that they have focused almost exclusively on rural environments. However, many of our evaluations take place in an urban setting. They do share some issues relevant to all deeply-buried sites, but also face a whole range of problems which are unique to their situation and which merit further research.

It is felt that the most useful aspect of the current study was the simulation of evaluation methods and sampling strategies on 'real' archaeology, sites scattered across the landscape where large gaps exist within settlements. A great deal of time was spent producing consistent and 'clean' digitally-based site plans, which reduced the time that could be spent undertaking simulations. More work could be undertaken profitably, using the dataset now available, to investigate more thoroughly the issues of variability in trench positioning, particular for the Saxon sites. With relatively little extra work a greater degree of statistical validity could be gained, and perhaps a better understanding of the problems of detecting Anglo-Saxon remains. This is particularly true for the wide variety of trenching arrays that were only modelled in totality on three sites. Similarly, a wider range of evaluation strategies could be simulated.

7   BIBLIOGRAPHY

Blakely, R J, 1995 *Potential Theory in Gravity and Magnetic Applications*, Cambridge University Press, Cambridge

Carver, M, 1987 *Underneath English Towns*, Batsford, London

Champion, T, Shennan, S and Cuming, P, 1995 *Planning for the past, volume III: decision-making and field methods in archaeological evaluation*, Southampton University and English Heritage, Southampton

Cherry, J F, Gamble, C, and Shennan, S, 1978 *Sampling in contemporary British archaeology*, BAR Brit Ser **50**, Oxford

Clark, A J, 1983 The testimony of the topsoil, in *The impact of aerial reconnaissance on Archaeology* (ed. G S Maxwell), CBA Res Rep **9**, 128-135, London

Clark, A J, 1996 *Seeing beneath the soil*, Batsford, London

Darvill, T, Burrow, S, and Wildgust, D, 1995 *Planning for the past, volume II: an assessment of archaeological assessments, 1982-91*, Bournemouth University and English Heritage, Bournemouth

English Heritage, 1995a *Planning for the past, volume I: a review of archaeological assessment procedures in England 1982-91*, English Heritage, London

English Heritage, 1995b Geophysical survey in Archaeological Field Evaluation, *Research and Professional Services Guideline* **1**, English Heritage, London

Goudswaard, B, forthcoming Archaeology within the Betuweroute, the Netherlands: case studies for the evaluation of strategies and priorities, in *Approaches to Archaeological Evaluation in England, Belgium (Flanders and Wallonia), France and the Netherlands*, (eds K Evans and J H Williams)

Hey, G, 1994 Yarnton-Cassington Project, a Neolithic to medieval landscape: project design, OAU and English Heritage Report, November 1994

Hey, G, 1998 The Yarnton-Cassington Project: evaluating a floodplain landscape, *Lithics* **19**, 47-60

Lewis, C, Mitchell-Fox, P, and Dyer, C 1997 *Village, hamlet and field: changing medieval settlements in central England*, Manchester University Press, Manchester

Medlycott, M, and Germany, M, 1994 Archaeological fieldwalking in Essex, 1985-93: interim results, *Essex Archaeology and History* **25**, 14-28

Neubauer, W, and Eder-Hinterleitner, A, 1997 3D-interpretation of postprocessed archaeological magnetic prospection data, *Archaeological Prospection* **4**, 191-206

Scollar, I, Tabbagh, A, Hesse, A, and Herzog, I, 1990 *Archaeological prospecting and remote sensing*, Cambridge University Press, Cambridge

Sheen, N P, and Aspinall, A, 1995 A simulation of anomalies to aid the interpretation of magnetic data, in *Computer applications and quantitative methods in archaeology 1993*, (eds J Wilcock and K Lockyear), BAR Int Ser **598**, 57-63, Oxford

Shennan, S, 1988 *Quantifying Archaeology*, Edinburgh University Press

Orton, C, 2000 *Sampling in archaeology*, Cambridge University Press, Cambridge

Pryor, F, French, C, Crowther, D, Gurney, D, Simpson, G and Taylor, M, 1985 *Archaeology and Environment in the Lower Welland Valley*, East Anglian Archaeology **27**

Waugh, K, forthcoming The application of predictive modelling and augering as techniques for the assessment and evaluation of archaeological sites in the Netherlands, in *Approaches to Archaeological Evaluation in England, Belgium (Flanders and Wallonia), France and the Netherlands*, (eds K Evans and J H Williams)

Williams, J, 1997 Curating research frameworks, *The Archaeologist* **28**, 5-7

Appendix 1: SITE QUESTIONNAIRE

Table A1.1 Questionnaire: initial information

Site name   **Site code**   **OAU No:**

Initial Info	
Site name	
County	
Grid ref	
Type of development	
Name of developer	
Size of development	
Name of Consultant Archaeologist if applicable	
Planning History	
Name of Curator	
Name of English Heritage Inspector	
Urban or rural	
Geology	
Topography	
Depth of overburden	
Recent land use	

Table A1.2 Questionnaire: desk-based assessment

Site name: **Site code**   **OAU No.**

Desk based assessment

Desk based assessment?	EIA	Other Date
Compiled by (Unit)		
Where are reports/availability		
Use of geotechnical data		
Sources used		APs - Swindon, Local Authority, Cambridge, Other SMR NMR OS Maps Tithe maps Enclosure and award Estate maps Doumentary sources VCH Walkover LB lists SAM lists Previous excavations/fieldwork reports Borehole logs Test pit logs Site surveys Geology maps Bibliographic references Policy Statements, research frameworks Local/Unitary development plans Constraints mapping Other
Impact assessment		Detailed Moderate Summary
What Mitigation suggested		Trench Geophysics Fieldwalking Watching Brief Metal detecting Test Pitting Development redesign Excavation Other
Conclusions		
Conclusions/Commentary OAU		

Notes

Table A1.3 Questionnaire: fieldwalking

Site name: **Site code**   **OAU No.**

Fieldwalking

Contracting Unit	
Availability of reports	Written
	Digital
	Original archive
Date start & finish	
Area covered	
% of whole site	
Survey intervals	
Collections units	
Results: No. of sites identified per period	NEO
	BA
	IA
	RO
	EMED
	MED
	PMED
	MOD
Results: Extent of sites per period	NEO
	BA
	IA
	RO
	EMED
	MED
	PMED
	MOD
Results: Density of finds per scatter per period?	NEO
	BA
	IA
	RO
	EMED
	MED
	PMED
	MOD
Recommendations	
Weather conditions	
Ground conditions	
Experience of personnel	

Table A1.4 Questionnaire: geophysical survey

Site name: **Site code**   **OAU No.**

Geophysics

Contracting Unit	
Availability of reports	Written Digital Original archive?
Date start & finish	
Type of geophysics	Mag sus Magnetometer Resistivity Radar Metal detecting
Area covered	
% of whole site	
Space between grid	
Distance between readings	Magnetometer Mag Sus-
Height of instrument	
Density of features	High Medium Low
Clarity of Results	Mag sus Magnetometer Resistivity Radar Metal detecting
Recommendations/Conc	
Ground conditions	
Weather conditions	
Calrity and accuracy of results - notes	

Table A1.5 Questionnaire: test pits and boreholes

Site name: **Site code**   **OAU No.**

Test pitting and Boreholes

Contracting Unit	
Availability of reports	Written Digital Original archive?
Date start & finish	
Area covered	
Purpose of pitting	
Number of test pits	
Size of test pits	
% of whole site	
Space between test pits	
Soil sieved	
Size of mesh	
Density of features	High Medium Low
Results: No. of sites identified per period	NEO BA IA RO EMED MED PMED MOD
Results: Extent of sites per period	NEO BA IA RO EMED MED PMED MOD
Weather conditions	
Recommendations	

Table A1.6 Questionnaire: trench evaluation

Site name: **Site code**   **OAU No.**

Trench evaluation

Contracting Unit	
Availability of reports	Written Digital Original archive
Date start & finish	
Total dev area	
Area covered by trenches in m^2	
% of whole site trenched	
Overall sampling rationale	
No. of trenches	
Trench size	
Trench intervals	
Trench arrays	
Excavation strategy	
Trench depth	
Depth of overburden	
Environmental sampling	
Density of features overall	High Medium Low
Density of features per period (high, medium, low)	NEO BA IA RO EMED MED PMED MOD
Main types of site evidence per period Settlement Burial Religious Urban Industrial Agricultural Other	Site Type NEO Site Type BA Site Type IA Site Type RO Site Type EMED Site Type MED Site Type PMED Site Type MOD
Main types of features per period Buildings Field System Graves Amorphous (ie pits, ditches, etc) Other	Site Type NEO Site Type BA Site Type IA Site Type RO Site Type EMED Site Type MED Site Type PMED Site Type MOD
Health & Safety constraints	
Ground conditions	
Weather conditions	

Site name: **Site code**   **OAU No.**

Excavation

Contracting Unit	
Availability of reports	Written Digital Original archive
Date start & fin	
Area covered	
% of whole site	
Overall excavation rationale	
Trench depth	
Depth/type of stratigraphy	Simple (ie a few intercutting features but not many) Medium Complex
Depth of overburden	
Density of features overall	High Medium Low
Density of features per period (high, medium, low)	NEO BA IA RO EMED MED PMED MOD
Main types of site evidence per period Settlement Burial Religious Urban Industrial Agricultural Other	Site Type NEO Site Type BA Site Type IA Site Type RO Site Type EMED Site Type MED Site Type PMED Site Type MOD
Main types of features per period Buildings Field System Graves Amorphous (ie pits, ditches, etc) Other	Site Type NEO Site Type BA Site Type IA Site Type RO Site Type EMED Site Type MED Site Type PMED Site Type MOD
State of preservation	Excellent Good Variable Poor
Ground conditions	
Weather conditions	
Health & Safety constraints	

Table A1.8: Questionnaire: watching brief

Site name: **Site code** **OAU No.**

Watching brief

Contracting Unit	
Availability of reports	Written
	Digital
	Original archive
Date start & fin	
Area covered	
% of whole site	
Findings	
Density of features overall	High
	Medium
	Low
Density of features per period (high, medium, low)	NEO
	BA
	IA
	RO
	EMED
	MED
	PMED
	MOD
Main types of site evidence per period Settlement Burial Religious Urban Industrial Agricultural Other	Site Type NEO
	Site Type BA
	Site Type IA
	Site Type RO
	Site Type EMED
	Site Type MED
	Site Type PMED
	Site Type MOD
Main types of features per period Buildings Field System Graves Amorphous (ie pits, ditches, etc) Other	Site Type NEO
	Site Type BA
	Site Type IA
	Site Type RO
	Site Type EMED
	Site Type MED
	Site Type PMED
	Site Type MOD
Health & Safety constraints	
Weather conditions	

Table A1.9 Questionnaire: other information

Site name: **Site code** **OAU No.**

Other 75

Major discoveries leading to delays	
Type of building redesign mitigation	
Client satisfaction	
Other	

Notes

Site name: **Site code** **OAU No.**

Decision making process

Lists of reports consulted

To come/need

Appendix 2: STUDY OF GEOPHYSICAL SURVEYS

by Neil Linford and Andrew David,
Archaeometry Branch, English Heritage Centre for Archaeology

A2.1   Introduction

This report aims to make a contribution to OAU's evaluation of archaeological decision-making processes and sampling strategies. Whilst the overall project assesses the role of all types of archaeological evaluation, the following concerns only the specific contribution of geophysical survey.

Geophysical survey usually involves the use of instruments at the ground surface which are sensitive to variations in the physical properties of the underlying soil, such as its magnetism and electrical conductivity. Such variations, mapped as 'anomalies', can be interpreted in terms of their likely archaeological origin, and thereby often provide an invaluable prediction of archaeological significance. The principals and practice of the various geophysical methods are well covered in the literature (eg Clark 1996; Scollar et al 1990), and in the journal Archaeological Prospection (1994 onwards). Formal guidance on the use of geophysical survey in archaeological evaluation has been provided by English Heritage (English Heritage 1995b).

Since the introduction of official planning guidance (Planning Policy Guidance Note 16) in 1990, the use of these methods to assist in the archaeological evaluation of development sites has become commonplace. Within England there are, at the time of writing, an estimated 18 commercial groups offering a roughly estimated total of 400 archaeological geophysical surveys per year. The majority of such surveys use magnetometers (with and without the support of magnetic susceptibility measurements), although resistivity meters are also in frequent use. Ground Penetrating Radar (GPR) is presently applied less commonly but its use is increasing, particularly in urban contexts.

The availability of co-extensive geophysical survey and excavation provides the opportunity to attempt an objective comparison of the relative 'success' of geophysical survey in a number of these cases. Unfortunately, owing to the difficulty of achieving consistency between datasets, and to the limited time available, the number of case studies subjected to this analysis has been very limited.

The objectives of the study were, therefore, to assess the effectiveness of the techniques and methodologies used in the location and characterisation the archaeological potential of the evaluation area and, where relevant, to highlight problems of the interpretation of the geophysical data.

A2.2   Limitations of the project

From the outset it was apparent that the meeting of these objectives would be subject to a number of limiting factors relating to sample size, sample bias and data consistency, as discussed below. A number of technical limitations also became apparent during the analysis and these are discussed in their turn, under the description of procedural considerations (Section A2.3.1).

A2.2.1   Sample size

An important consideration in geophysical survey, as for archaeological evaluation more generally, is the fact that so many variables can interact to affect an outcome. An objective study ought, therefore, to include a large sample of situations in which the interplay of various critical parameters can be more fully assessed. For geophysical survey, some obvious parameters include geology, surface conditions, overburden, recent land-use and seasonality. The current study uses only a very small number of surveys that do not adequately cover the full range of variation normally encountered in evaluations.

A2.2.2 Sample bias

The case studies reviewed below are predominantly of magnetometer survey only. Resistivity survey was conducted at only one site, and there are no examples of the use of GPR. Furthermore, none of the case studies allow an assessment of geophysical and geochemical reconnaissance (such as magnetometer scanning and magnetic susceptibility survey). This report, therefore, cannot contribute to the persisting debate, which is reflected by an uncertainty amongst the wider archaeological community, concerning the efficacy of these various additional techniques. The potential contribution of geophysical methods to the evaluation of urban sites cannot be addressed either.

A2.2.3 Data consistency

None of the sample of geophysical surveys was conducted with a subsequent comparative analysis in mind, and there are, therefore, significant inconsistencies between the resulting datasets. One particular difficulty is the spatial correlation between the geophysical survey and subsequent excavation grids. Ideally, for such a comparative exercise physical fiducial grid markers would be established following the geophysical survey so that any identified anomalies may be related to underlying archaeological features with a high degree of relative accuracy. However, in general geophysical survey data is only located to local permanent markers (where these exist) and to the Ordnance Survey NGR to a suggested accuracy of at least 0.1 m and 1.0m respectively (English Heritage 1995b). For the current study, therefore, it has been assumed that a successful correlation between a significant anomaly and a subsequently excavated feature has occurred when these overlap within a buffer-zone of up to 2 m around the feature concerned.

A2.3   The analysis

Of the 12 evaluations initially considered, and taking into account constraints of time and data quality, the geophysical surveys of five sites were used in this comparative study (Table A2.1).

Whilst it is accepted that survey performance and the subsequent interpretation of the data may vary between practitioners, this study makes no attempt to assess these variables. The identities of the practitioners concerned have been omitted.

A2.3.1 Procedural considerations

It is important to consider the relationship between a geophysical anomaly within a dataset and the underlying causative feature. This relationship is based upon both the physical properties of the feature itself (eg size, fabric, depth of burial) and the geophysical methodology deployed. For example, the same archaeological feature may produce very different geophysical anomalies in magnetometer data than those recorded over the same area by a resistivity survey. Even minor alteration of survey procedure, such as sampling interval or instrument operating parameters may produce significantly different anomalies from the same survey area.

Much research has been conducted into the theoretical prediction of geophysical anomalies and the numerical treatment of survey data to provide a resolved image

Table A2.1 The Sites and the surveys

Site	Survey(1)	Instruments	Sampling(2)	Area	Geology	Conditions
Westhawk Farm	Mag	Geoscan FM36	0.5m x 1.0m	10ha	Weald clay	Arable fields with cereal crops at varying stages of maturity throughout the survey visits
Yarnton Cresswell Field	Mag	Geoscan FM36	0.25m x 1.0m	3.5ha	River terrace gravel	Arable field with germinating cereal crop
Yarnton Site 5	Mag	Geoscan FM36	0.25m x 1.0m	0.9ha	Alluvium overlying river terrace gravel	Arable field with germinating cereal crop, considerable ferrous detritus in the topsoil
Thurnham Roman Villa	Mag	Geoscan FM36	?0.5m x 1.0m	1.0ha	Calcareous soils overlying Chalk and Gault clay	Arable field with germinating cereal crop
	Res	Geoscan RM15 (0.5m Twin Electrode)	1.0m x 1.0m	1.0ha		
Thanet Way	Mag	Geoscan FM36	0.33m x 1.0m	approx 3.5ha	Brickearth, mainly Loess overlying Chalk	

(1) Survey type: Mag = Fluxgate Magnetometer, Res = Earth Resistance survey
(2) Sample interval: X x Y where X is the sample interval along parallel transects separated by Y, all measurements in metres
For earth resistance surveys the electrode configuration and electrode spacing is also included

that more closely describes the physical characteristics of the underlying feature (Sheen and Aspinall 1995; Neubauer and Eder-Hinterleitner 1997). However, such analysis is complex and often requires considerable a priori assumptions to be made regarding the likely features to be encountered on a particular site. The current procedure for interpreting geophysical data from evaluations is more subjective still, and largely depends simply upon the experience of the interpreter in the recognition and delineation of apparently significant anomalies. The majority of geophysical survey data is usually accompanied by a summary interpretation which takes into account all the available datasets as well as the influence of the instrumentation and survey parameters used.

Whilst the aim of this study is to provide a semi-quantitative assessment of the effectiveness of geophysical survey over a range of different sites it should be re-emphasised that the available data was not collected, at the time, with this specific purpose in mind. Moreover, the scope of the current study has had to be restricted to a simple comparison of geophysical anomalies from the summary interpretation plans with the location of subsequently excavated archaeological features. These interpretations have all been derived from a thorough examination of the geophysical data and were produced in a digital geo-referenced format. However, a degree of inconsistency within the interpretation procedure is inevitable due to the differing practices of the survey teams involved (see above). It should be noted, however, that the data from all the sites under consideration met with a consistently high standard.

The semi-quantitative evaluation of geophysical data is by no means a trivial matter and the following limitations should be considered:

Variation in topography: in general, the topography of the ground surface when the geophysical surveys were conducted will differ from the underlying excavated surface. This difference may be further exacerbated by the presence of a crop or foliage during the geophysical fieldwork. Whilst such variation is often subtle, it may account for a considerable (0.5-1.0 m) displacement between points, usually assumed to be co-located, within the survey and subsequent excavation.

Survey grid: it is standard practice for geophysical survey grids to be established at a convenient orientation to surface obstacles, such as field boundaries, to enable the rapid acquisition of survey data. Where accurate tie-in measurements are not available, the subsequent re-location of the survey grid by measurements to landmarks mapped by the Ordnance Survey can only be accurate to approximately 1m. The location of excavation trenches, perhaps on a different orientation to the geophysical survey grid, may contain a similar degree of error. In addition, the survey grid (and the resulting geophysical data) is seldom corrected for variations introduced by minor positional errors over undulating terrain.

Displacement of geophysical anomalies: it is important to be aware that geophysical anomalies generally cover both a greater area and may be offset from the precise location of the underlying causative feature. Whilst data reduction routines may be applied to correct for such displacements (eg reduction to the pole, Blakely 1995) the error involved is often marginal and may be included within the graphical portrayal of anomalies within the interpretation plan.

Digitisation errors: digitised versions of both the geophysical interpretation plan and the excavation plan were required to enable spatial analysis within a Geographic Information System (GIS). Again, the available data was not necessarily collected with this procedure in mind and a certain degree of subjective "data cleaning" was required to produce data consisting entirely of closed polygons rather than open lines. As the original site drawings were not available a number of features remain unresolved as unclosed polygons and have therefore been excluded from the analysis. In addition, the resolution of raster-based images derived from the original vector data was limited to a pixel size of 0.5 m for computational efficiency.

Fidelity of the archaeological data: all the geophysical data was compared to the excavation data on the assumption that the latter was an absolute record of the presence or absence of archaeological features. However, a number of potentially significant magnetic anomalies did not correlate with recorded features – a phenomenon which may be explained by the presence of highly ephemeral concentrations of more magnetic material in the near-surface overlooked during excavation (cf Clark 1983; 1996).

A2.3.2 Statistical procedures

Taking the above limitations into account a statistical procedure was developed for the spatial analysis of the geophysical data sets with respect to the subsequently excavated features. First, geo-referenced datasets for both the geophysical interpretation and the subsequent excavation plan in a vector format were imported into the GIS (GRASS v4.3). Raster images were then derived from the original vector data to enable the degree of correlation between the two datasets to be established using the following classification scheme:

True Positive
Indicates a direct correlation between a geophysical anomaly identified in the interpretation plan and subsequently excavated archaeological feature. This classification is calculated from a 2 m buffer-zone around the archaeological features to account for the positional inaccuracies noted above. The data is thus subdivided into five bins representing the distance from the geophysical anomaly to the nearest recorded feature from 0.0 m (direct overlap) through 0.5, 1.0, 1.5, and 2.0 m. The data is presented as the areas covered by geophysical anomalies falling with these classifications, normalised by the total area of geophysical anomalies within the interpretation plan.

False Positive
This classification refers to those geophysical anomalies within the excavated area that failed to correlate with a subsequently recorded archaeological feature within

the same 2 m buffer. The statistic is again presented as a percentage of the total area covered by geophysical anomalies and is equal to 1 – True Positive.

True Negative
This classification attempts to quantify the ability of the geophysical survey to accurately identify areas containing no archaeological activity. It is calculated as a percentage area beyond the 2 m buffer surrounding the archaeological features containing no False Positive geophysical anomalies. However, an additional weighting term has been introduced based on the area ratio of identified anomalies to subsequently recorded archaeological features. This was necessary in order to avoid a misleadingly high percentage for True Negative in circumstances where a geophysical interpretation contained few, if any, positive anomalies. It is important to remember that the True Negative statistic provides a relative score for inter-comparison between the datasets opposed to the percentage area of the site devoid of archaeological activity.

False Negative
All recorded archaeological features that failed to produce a significant geophysical anomaly within a 2 m buffer are recorded in this classification, presented as a percentage of the total area of excavated features.

The data, as classified above, is presented both numerically (Table A2.2) and as a series of false colour raster images superimposed over the underlying excavation plan (Figs 39-43). For the reasons discussed in the introduction, the analysis is restricted only to recorded magnetometer and resistivity survey. No attempt is made here to assess methods of geophysical pilot survey or reconnaissance.

A2.4   Results

The following section briefly summarises the circumstances of each geophysical survey and attempts to assess the relative merits of the results in each case, within the broader context of the subsequent excavations.

A2.4.1   Westhawk Farm

Following the results of encouraging magnetic scanning, a large-scale magnetometer survey was conducted in three separate visits during January-December 1996, April-May 1997 and February 1998. The site consists of predominately silty and/or loamy clay drift soils of the Whickam 1 Association overlying Cretaceous clay or mudstone, and ground conditions were rolled arable fields with a germinating cereal crop. Roman burials had been discovered during pipe-laying across the site and there was also evidence for the course of a Roman road.

The combined magnetic data identified a wide range of anomalies that were subsequently confirmed through excavation (Fig. 39). Many anomalies were related to linear ditch-type features, such as the flanking ditches of the Roman road. However, a large number of pit-type and semi-industrial thermoremanent anomalies were also correctly identified. It is interesting to the note that some of the slighter features, particularly to the south-west of the site, failed to produce significant magnetic anomalies. The lack of ditch anomalies in this area, well over a hectare in size and shown to include many ditches, may apparently be attributable to the presence of a crop on this part of the site at the time of the survey. The need to hold the magnetometer sensors at a higher level from the ground may have contributed to the poorer definition here. Further to the north, the gully ditches of the temple enclosure were only partially replicated in the magnetic data and no geophysical evidence for the internal timber circle was found. In addition, a number of linear magnetic anomalies are clearly aligned with the course of excavated ditches but were not, apparently, related to an observed feature in the field.

Table A2.2 Results of analysis of geophysical survey

Site	True (False) Positive			True Negative	False Negative
Westhawk Farm (magnetometer)	80.7% (19.3%)	0m 0.5m 1.0 1.5m 2.0m	32.7% 18.5% 13.4% 9.9% 6.2%	35.1%	52.4%
Yarnton Cresswell Field (magnetometer)	83.3% (16.7%)	0m 0.5m 1.0 1.5m 2.0m	30.3% 21.1% 16.4% 9.8% 5.7%	61.5%	20.4%
Yarnton Site 5 (magnetometer)	71.6% (28.4%)	0m 0.5m 1.0 1.5m 2.0m	52.3% 8.4% 5.2% 1.6% 4.1%	57.0%	21.3%
Thurnham Roman Villa (resistivity)	65.5% (34.5%)	0m 0.5m 1.0 1.5m 2.0m	25.8% 15.6% 8.8% 8.7% 6.6%	66.4%	39.3%
Thurnham Roman Villa (magnetometer)	58.9% (41.1%)	0m 0.5m 1.0 1.5m 2.0m	13.9% 15.4% 12.9% 9.5% 7.2%	36.4%	78.4%
Thanet Way (magnetometer)	74.3% (25.7%)	0m 0.5m 1.0 1.5m 2.0m	49.6% 8.1% 6.5% 6.2% 3.9%	86.9%	45.3%

Perhaps of greater concern are the results from the excavation trench opened to the north of the main site. Here the geophysical data contains only a scatter of non-linear responses and has failed to indicate the ditch system revealed by excavation. Whilst the geophysical data has correctly indicated the presence of archaeological activity it is questionable whether the significance of the remains in this area would have been appreciated from the survey data alone.

It would appear from the geophysical results that the magnetic response gradually diminishes from the centre of the site to edge of the survey area. This may in part be due to the topography of the site, sloping gently downhill from the centre, leading to a greater depth of colluvial overburden. However, topsoil magnetic susceptibility values recorded during the survey demonstrate enhanced susceptibility in the vicinity of semi-industrial, thermoremanent features. It may be suggested that the magnetic fill of cut features at the site is derived from their proximity to such features and therefore that other activity remote from this (and from associated settlement) is less likely to produce distinguishable magnetic anomalies. Whilst topsoil magnetic susceptibility surveys have not been included within this study (due to a lack of suitable data) this site demonstrates how such information could be used to aid the interpretation of the magnetometer survey.

A2.4.2 *Yarnton Cresswell Field*

This site lies on a substrate of Oxford Clay and Kellaways Beds overlain by deposits of Postglacial river gravel from the second (Summertown-Radley) terrace. Fine loamy soils of the Badsey 1 Association have developed over the gravel with more clay-rich soils found along the course of a buried palaeochannel crossing the site to the north. Fluxgate gradiometer data was collected over ~4ha during March 1995

0.0	
0.5	
1.0	True Positive
1.5	
2.0m	
	False Positive
	False Negative

0 ■■■■■■■■ 90m

Figure 39 Westhawk Farm: archaeological features superimposed over a false colour image illustrating spatial analysis of the geophysical survey interpretation

followed by the subsequent excavation of ~2ha of the total area. A germinating winter cereal crop was present in the field at the time of the survey.

The survey revealed a plethora of magnetic anomalies, including responses to both the palaeochannel and a remnant ridge-and-furrow cultivation pattern (Fig. 40). The latter responses, although correctly identified, have been excluded from the analysis. More significant pit-, ditch- and enclosure-anomalies were also revealed that correlated with subsequently excavated archaeological features from the Neolithic/early Bronze Age to the post-medieval periods. Within the resulting palimpsest of anomalies there was little variation of response with respect to period and only the slighter posthole type features failed to be replicated in the magnetic data. In particular, four early Iron Age hut circles and an Anglo-Saxon building, reconstructed only from a pattern of excavated postholes, were not identified in the survey data.

It is noticeable that many anomalies, despite a true positive attribution, are offset to some degree (up to several metres in places) from their causative features. This is attributed to topographic variation (see above) and illustrates the problems that this can introduce. Although the resulting offsets have not compromised the general evaluation of the archaeological potential of the site in this case, they nevertheless raise a concern for other evaluations which might require a more accurate location of specific features.

It is of interest to note that the magnetic survey failed to completely detect a substantial medieval field-boundary ditch crossing the site north-south on the same alignment as the ridge and furrow. This feature was certainly substantial enough to be detected by the magnetometer and has not been over-cut by any later archaeological activity. Its apparent lack of magnetic enhancement is difficult to explain given the magnitude of response demonstrated by the ridge and furrow and suggests a later phase of less intense activity at the site.

A2.4.3   Yarnton Site 5

This fluxgate gradiometer survey was conducted during November 1993 following a 2% trial trenching evaluation of the Yarnton floodplain prior to mineral extraction. Geological conditions, although superficially similar to Yarnton Cresswell Field, were more challenging as this lower-lying site on the floodplain is overlain and complicated by a deposit of more recent alluvium of varying thickness. Clayey soils of the Thames and Kelmscot Associations have developed over the alluvium and are affected by groundwater and seasonal waterlogging. Ground conditions were arable, down to the production of winter cereal, with a significant quantity of ferrous detritus within the topsoil due to the recent practice of incorporating domestic refuse screened from an organic waste-processing plant operated by the landowner close to the site.

Despite such unfavourable conditions magnetic survey had proved fruitful over similar terrain in the project area and was considered at Site 5 following the discovery of a Neolithic enclosure ditch during trial trenching (Fig. 41). Data from the site contained numerous high intensity 'iron spikes' due to the concentration of ferrous litter but after the removal of these, the resultant data fell within a range of ±0.5nT, close to the practical noise limit of the gradiometer. However, a weak positive anomaly was revealed that described an incomplete rectilinear 30 m ? 60 m enclosure truncated by the field boundary to the east. The fidelity of this anomaly was corroborated through subsequent area excavation that identified it as caused by a rare Neolithic funerary enclosure. Due to the extremely weak nature of this anomaly the full outline of the enclosure, that was continuous save for a single break in the southern branch of the ditch, could not be determined from the geophysical data alone.

A number of more tentative pit-type anomalies were also identified in the magnetic data and these showed a reasonable correlation with some of the excavated features. Unfortunately, the interpretation of such relatively small features was severely hampered by the ferrous detritus, particularly within the area of the enclosure itself.

A2.4.4   Thurnham Villa

Both magnetometer and resistivity surveys were carried out in January-February 1995 over an area of approximately 1 hectare on calcareous soils overlying Chalk and Gault Clay. The ground conditions were arable, consisting of a germinating

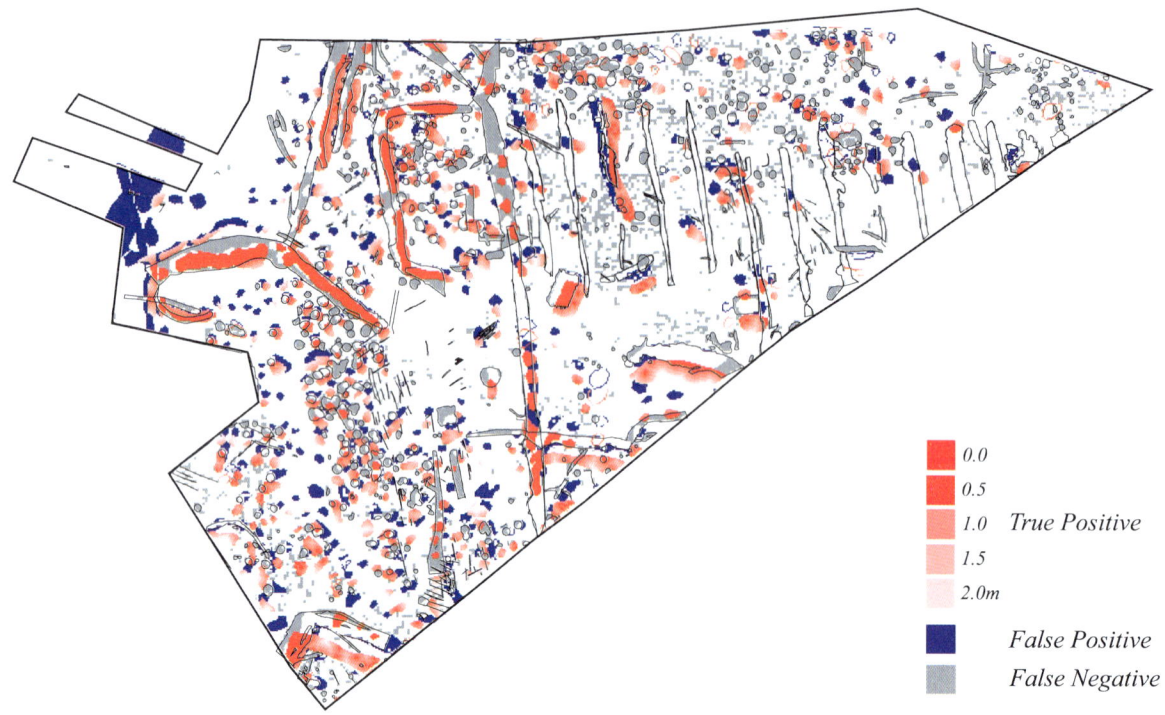

0.0
0.5
1.0 *True Positive*
1.5
2.0m

False Positive
False Negative

Figure 40 Yarnton Cresswell Field: archaeological features superimposed over a false colour image illustrating spatial analysis of the geophysical survey interpretation

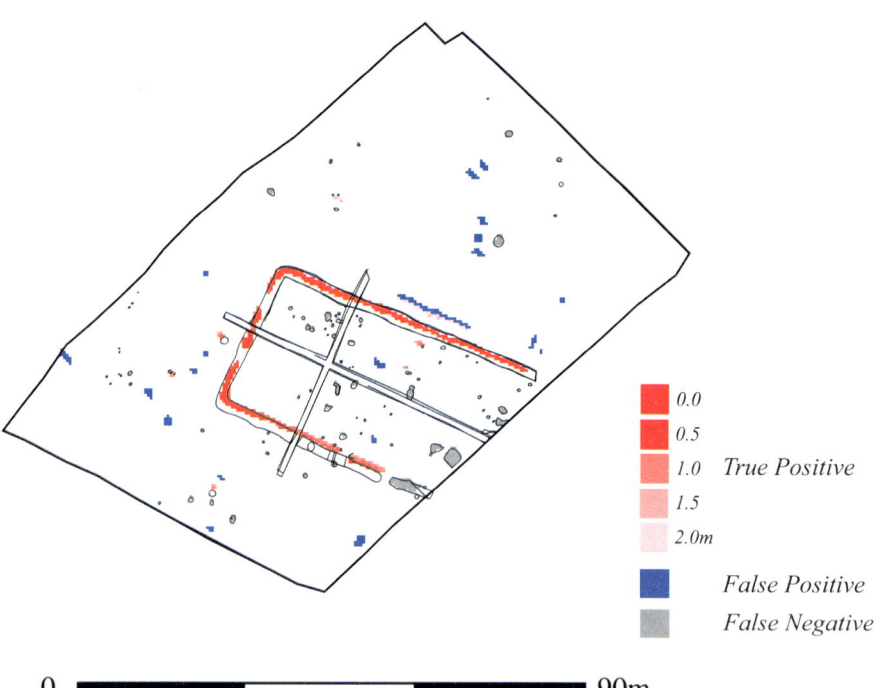

0.0
0.5
1.0 *True Positive*
1.5
2.0m

False Positive
False Negative

0 ▬▬▬▬▬▬▬▬ 90m

Figure 41 Yarnton Site 5: archaeological features superimposed over a false colour image illustrating spatial analysis of the geophysical survey interpretation

cereal crop. The presence of a Roman building was already known from aerial photographic evidence and previous excavation.

The resistivity survey successfully located the known Roman building and also found a previously unknown and substantial aisled building (Fig. 42). Other resistivity anomalies were indeterminate, with a varied response to ditch-type anomalies of all phases across the survey area. It is of interest to note the offset between the geophysical anomalies within the aisled building and the location of the excavated features. This appears more pronounced following the southern colonnade of column bases and is difficult to explain within such a small area (see above). Other more tentative linear anomalies identified by the resistivity survey did not correlate with excavated features. (Due to the use of a 2 m buffer-zone around the excavated

Magnetometer

Resistivity

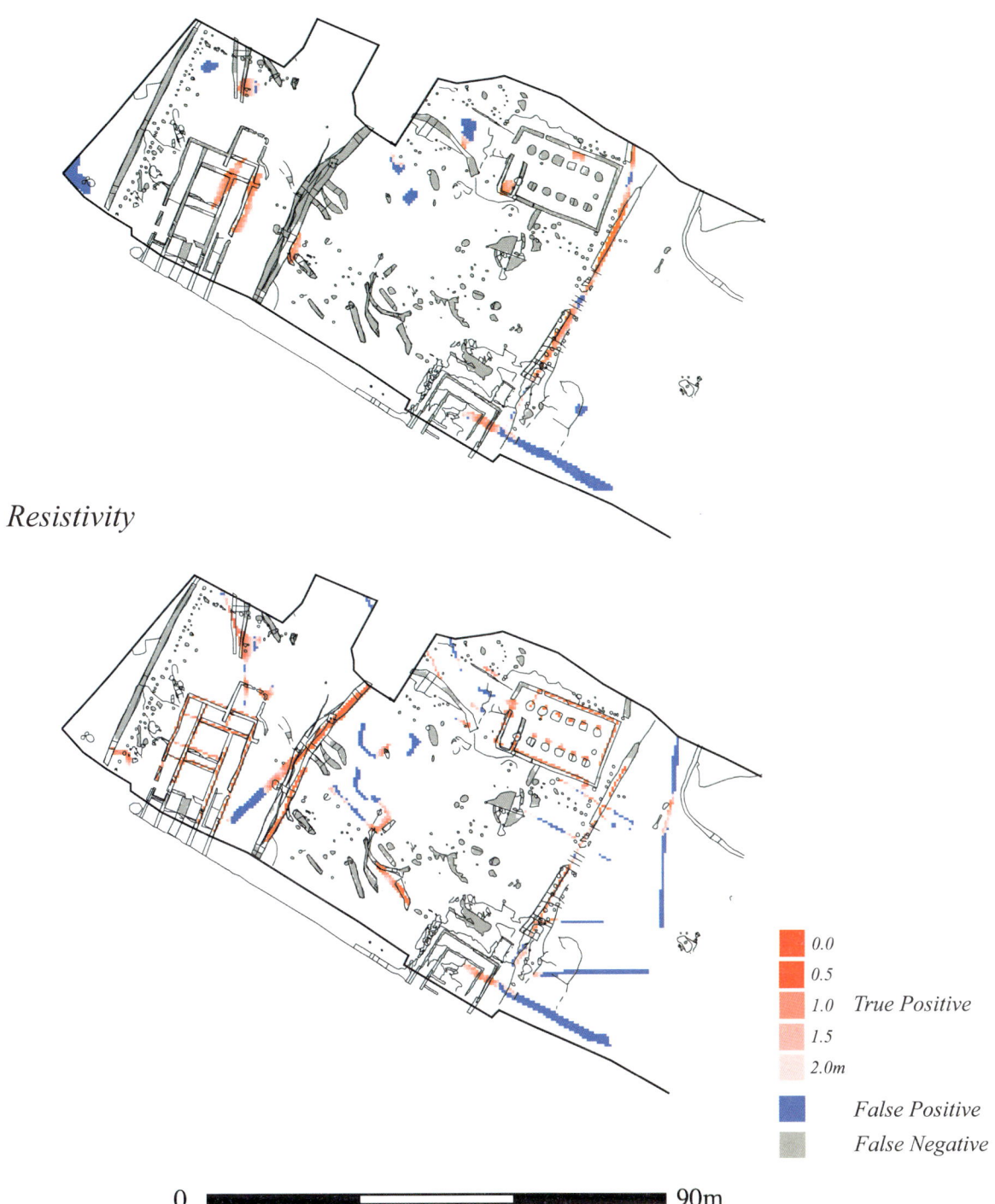

■	0.0
■	0.5
■	1.0 *True Positive*
■	1.5
■	2.0m
■	*False Positive*
■	*False Negative*

0 ▬▬▬▬▬▬▬▬▬▬▬▬▬▬▬▬▬▬ 90m

Figure 42 Thurnham Roman Villa: archaeological features superimposed over a false colour image illustrating spatial analysis of the geophysical survey interpretation

features a number of spurious anomalies have been mistakenly credited as true positives because they fall within the 2 m zone of unrelated features. This effect does not, however, remove the possibility that such anomalies may have been genuine near-surface features unrecognised by excavation).

The magnetometer response at the site was comparatively unhelpful, being dominated by scatters of many isolated anomalies some of which were broadly coincident with resistivity anomalies, but without obvious patterning. One linear anomaly was interpreted as a possible boundary ditch, confirmed by the subsequent excavation. However, no magnetic anomalies (positive or negative) were generated by the wall footings of the Roman buildings. Two substantial thermoremanent anomalies were recorded in the vicinity of the buildings but it is questionable whether these would have been correctly identified without the accompanying excavation. Unfortunately, a number of magnetic anomalies, including large amorphous areas of disturbance, lie beyond the area of the subsequent excavation (and thus of the statistical analysis) and their significance cannot be assessed.

A2.4.5 *Thanet Way*

This 1992 magnetometer survey took place along the course of a road widening corridor extending for some 2.5 km across mainly arable land, over Chalk. Supplementary magnetic susceptibility measurements were made on soil samples collected at 20 m intervals. Aerial photographs showed the presence of a number of features, such as ring ditches, and subsequent excavation covered the entire development, although the following analysis is based on a reduced ~1.2 km length of the road corridor. The geophysical results were provided as a series of A0 greytone/trace plots of the magnetometer and magnetic susceptibility surveys together with a text report. No graphical summary of significant geophysical anomalies was available and so this was produced by the Centre for Archaeology directly from the data plots and then digitised by OAU for the GIS analysis.

It is possible that this procedure has led to the offset between the location of geophysical anomalies and subsequently excavated features that becomes progressively greater from east to west across the excavated area. However, this is felt to be improbable and that the offsets are more likely to be due to a topographic discrepancy between the modern ground surface and the excavation surfaces. In keeping with the other datasets included within this study, no attempt has been made to rectify the location of the geophysical anomalies to the excavated features.

The site demonstrates a good magnetic response to the presence of ditches and pits along the entire course of the road corridor with ring ditches and trackways showing clearly (Fig. 43). However, timber buildings were not identified, nor were small features such as postholes and post-in-slot buildings. This may be due to the weak response of these features and the presence of considerable cultural noise in areas of the survey due to buried services and passing traffic. In addition, a preferential detection of east-west orientated anomalies is evident within the data due, no doubt, to the direction (north-south) of the survey traverses along which the data were collected.

Analysis of the magnetic susceptibility survey is beyond the scope of the current study, as the technique does not provide sufficient resolution to identify discrete anomalies, when applied at a 20 m sample interval. However, the results of the MS survey have been used to complement the interpretation of the magnetometer data, for example to indicate the possible location of masonry buildings. In general, increased topsoil susceptibility was found to correlate with the presence of archaeological activity and the presence of significant magnetometer anomalies along the corridor.

A2.5 Discussion

Very limited though this analysis has been, its results fully sustain the fact that geophysical survey can be an extremely valuable and cost-effective means of site evaluation, where ground conditions are suitable and appropriate methodologies are adopted. Of four of the evaluations considered above, and assuming a margin of error of up to 2 m, over 70% of the identified magnetometer anomalies correlated with subsequently excavated features. Of these anomalies, over 50% fell within 0.5 m of the respective excavated feature, attesting to the accuracy obtainable with this technique when applied at an appropriate sample interval. At Thurnham, where resistivity has been used as well, it is clear that this method was, at least in this case,

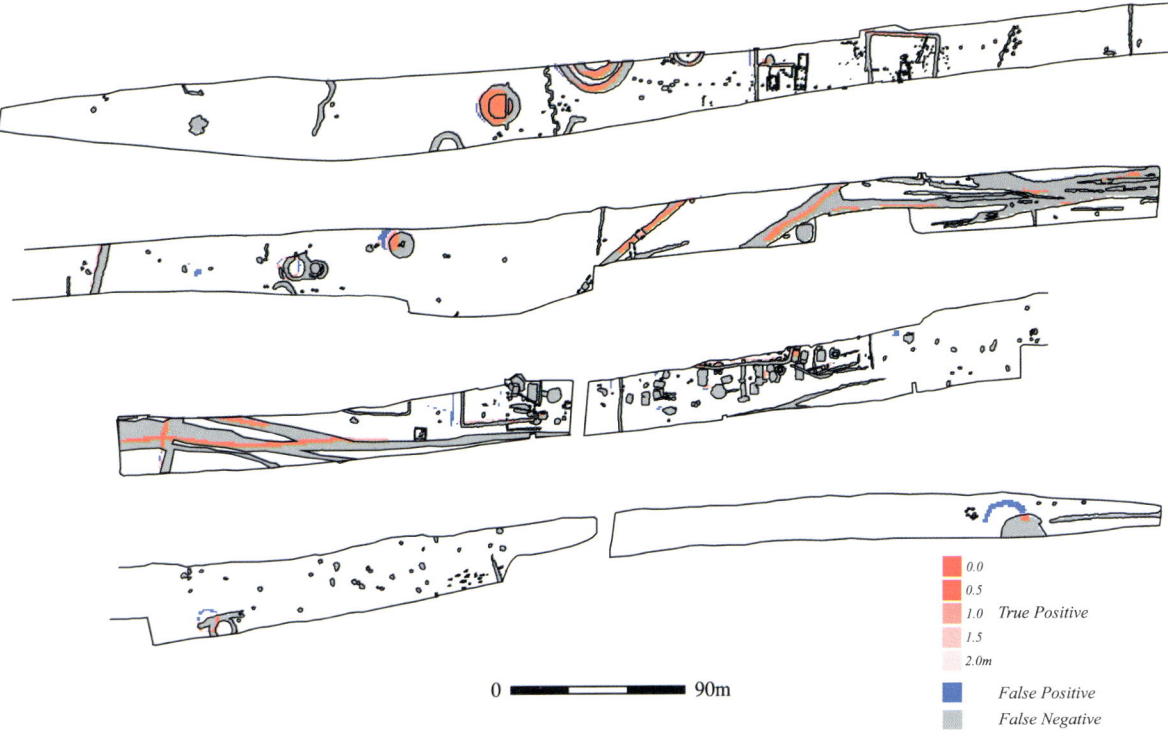

Figure 43 Thanet Way: archaeological features superimposed over a false colour image illustrating spatial analysis of the geophysical survey interpretation

better adapted to locating building foundations rather than the more substantial ditches and thermoremanent features to which the magnetometer responded better. 65.5% of the identified resistivity anomalies correlated with subsequently excavated features, including a previously unknown building.

The ability of geophysical survey to correctly identify areas with no significant archaeological activity is of equal importance to this study. Geophysical data alone cannot usually be used to support the concept of negative evidence - that is, that a site without anomalies is therefore without archaeological significance. The evidence from the above analysis is equivocal on this issue, showing that areas with no geophysical anomalies that correctly correspond with an absence of features vary from 35.1% to 86.9% across the five sites (Table A2.2). It would appear that these figures are influenced both by the density of archaeological remains and by the inability of the geophysical techniques, and the sample intervals applied, to identify smaller features such as postholes and small pits. Where such features are located in proximity to other more readily detectable features they are likely to be identified during subsequent invasive evaluation; but, it is nonetheless clear (as exemplified by the temple and enclosure at Westhawk Farm; Fig. 39) that geophysical data can and does overlook very important remains. These results confirm a significant limitation of geophysical survey that must not be dismissed, and they emphasise the need for appropriate specification of methodology and the exercise of considerable caution in any dismissal of significance where no anomalies are evident.

These observations aside, the assessment of the efficacy of geophysical survey must take account of a number of highly influential factors, as discussed below.

A2.5.1 The survey objectives

The objectives of survey may conveniently be divided into two general types:

Firstly, there is the search survey, which is intended to explore for any archaeological features within the development area. Usually there are already indications (eg from air photographs, artefact scatters, etc) that the area is archaeologically significant. This type of survey usually takes place after desk-top assessment, but before trial trenching. The survey results are usually expected to inform the disposition of evaluation trenches and may influence subsequent excavation strategies. Most geophysical evaluations, including those case studies considered above, are of this type.

A primary consideration of such reconnaissance surveys must be the fact that they are not usually required to provide a highly resolved and precisely located plan (or period attribution) of most buried features. Usually, such a survey may be deemed to have been sufficiently successful, as an evaluation exercise, if it has provided a reliable general indication of an archaeological presence and character as well as an approximate location.

Secondly, there is a more precise type of survey, designed to locate specific features prior to trial trenching or excavation, or to provide supplementary information after such interventions. This type of survey is possibly a less frequent requirement of evaluations than the more general search survey.

Many geophysical surveys will, of course, combine both motives , the Thurnham Villa site being a good example. The more general search surveys are typified by the work undertaken at Westhawk Farm, Yarnton, and Thanet Way. The point to make here is that the objectives of geophysical survey will vary from one evaluation site to another, depending on a number of factors. It follows that each geophysical survey needs to be judged according to its particular circumstances – which will differ from site to site. It is therefore probably unrealistic to attempt a universally applicable definition of a successful survey and there is a risk that isolated statistical parameters may be misleading; the definition of 'success' is too variable.

A2.5.2   The interpretation of geophysical survey data

Despite recent attempts to develop the theory and software capable of an objective definition of targets in geophysical data, the interpretation of such data remains an essentially subjective exercise. The current trend in the reporting of geophysical surveys is for the inclusion of a summary interpretation plan which indicates, by the use of varying graphical conventions, the outline or area of anomalies judged to be archaeologically significant (and those that are obviously not). There is no agreed convention for the presentation of such interpretations, and the niceties by which they can be presented and described by an accompanying text, are extremely variable, being heavily dependent on the particular experience and preconceptions of the specialist concerned. The varying 'freedom' with which anomalies are interpreted adds a further major complication to any attempts at a consistent and objective comparison between surveys and subsequent archaeological findings.

Similarly, any attempt to provide a statistical analysis of such data will be highly subjective. In the present study the emphasis has been placed on the assessment of the supplied geophysical interpretations as an aid to archaeological evaluation. The process does not consider either the quality of the data, which was considered to be beyond reproach in these cases, or the efficacy of the interpretation procedure that led to the identification of anomalies. In addition, no attempt has been made to rectify or otherwise alter the geophysical data in light of information that would only be available following excavation. This was thought to provide a more objective assessment of the geophysical techniques within the context of archaeological evaluation.

A2.6 Conclusions

This analysis of the effectiveness of geophysical survey has suffered from a number of significant limitations imposed by circumstance. There can be little doubt of the continuing requirement for a larger study utilising specifically dedicated datasets, much greater breadth of sampling (both of sites, geologies and techniques) and a more developed spatial analysis – for instance inclusion of quantitative analysis by period. Despite this need, the case studies reported here at least provide some fundamental conclusions which seem likely to hold good further afield.

First and foremost is the resounding endorsement of the fact that, in the right conditions, and correctly applied, geophysical methods are indeed highly effective at locating archaeological features. This ability was not tested in urban surroundings, or over areas with very deep overburden, but their poor performance in these latter circumstances is not yet disputable. However, in the type of conditions represented by the five rural sites analysed above, the efficacy of the methodology cannot be in doubt. The value of magnetometry as the technique most responsive to the greater range of features is confirmed, as is the better ability of resistivity to locate building foundations. In both cases there is a good degree of correlation between prediction, based on geophysical anomalies, and the outcome of subsequent excavation.

The analysis has revealed that interpreted anomalies are often horizontally displaced from the actual positions of the features responsible for them. This displacement seems likely to be the combined result of errors introduced by topographic variation and variations in depth between the ground surface and the causative feature. Whether or not such displacements significantly detract from the success of the survey depends upon the latter's objective. If this is a simple reconnaissance-type survey intended to provide a general indication of archaeological activity and character then perhaps locational errors of about 2 m are not a major concern. The problem of displacement becomes more acute for those surveys which require a higher level of spatial correlation with features, and our results suggest the exercise of caution on these occasions, particularly where sites are topographically variable. Data reduction routines (such as reduction to the pole for magnetic data) seem only to provide marginal improvements in positional accuracy, probably less significant than errors introduced by topography. The displacement of anomalies, and their possible rectification, is certainly an area which would benefit from further study.

Whilst geophysical survey is so clearly a valuable approach in field evaluations, this analysis has emphasised the continuing need to be alert to the fact that many types of small-scale or subtle features are undetectable. This deficiency may again be of less significance if other related features are detectable, but it must remain a cardinal rule that absence of anomalies does not necessarily imply an absence of significant features. Conversely (but much more rarely) the absence of features need not invalidate certain anomalies, as some causative features may be too ephemeral to be easily observed during excavation.

It now remains for more comprehensive studies, ever more feasible in the new era of geo-referenced data, to develop these comparative analyses a great deal further. In the meantime much of the above will not come as a surprise to those familiar with geophysical evaluation in field archaeology; but it has at least been useful to have this opportunity to repeat the stipulation that "Geophysical survey should be thought of as one of the main techniques of site evaluation and its potential contribution should be considered in each instance where development is proposed" (English Heritage 1995b).

Appendix 3: DETAILED METHODOLOGY OF THE COMPUTER SIMULATIONS, AND THEIR RESULTS

A3.1 Preparing sites for computer simulations

The difficulties of creating digitally-based plans of the sites in this study, and of differentiating between the various archaeological phases present, has already been discussed in the main text (Section 2.1.3). The creation of such composite drawings obviously relies on geo-referencing the original plans, and for those drawings where co-ordinates were not shown, other map data was used to locate, scale, and orientate the various drawings.

A3.2 Trenching array simulations

A3.2.1 Preparation of trenching models

The trenching arrays selected for simulation from the numerous possible configurations are described in Section 4.1, and illustrated on Figure 20. For each type of trench array, at each different sample fraction, an AutoCAD file was created consisting of a large array of trenches, designed to be big enough to cover the extents of any of the sites to be analysed. In order to do this, a single trench of the appropriate size was precisely created using the AutoCAD 2000's 'rectangle' command. Having calculated the area covered by this single trench, the area of which it was 2% (for example) could be deduced. This larger area could then be drawn, and the single trench positioned at its centre, to create a representation of an evaluation trench and its 'hinterland'. Copies of this area and trench could then be made, and moved or rotated as necessary, in order to create the basic repeating unit of the array. The AutoCAD 'array' function could then be used to multiply this drawing of a single 'unit', until the required size was reached. When the desired array had been created, the superfluous 'areas' could be deleted from the drawing, leaving only the trench arrangement.

A3.2.2 Positioning of the trench arrays

Following their creation, each individual trench array drawing could then be inserted as a scaled block into any of the digital site drawings, in order to create a simulation.

The site plan at that stage had all its archaeological layers turned off, leaving only the outline, so that the actual positioning of the trench array could not be influenced (consciously or sub-consciously) by the archaeological remains. As an extra precaution the drawing would also be zoomed out so that the site outline would be barely visible. In this way, each trench array could be modelled, without any fear that the final position of the individual trenches could be influenced in any way by the experimenter's knowledge of the archaeology present on the site.

After inserting the array of trenches, the array was usually rotated to a suitable alignment with respect to site boundaries, as is common in practice. For example, assuming no a priori knowledge about the likely alignment of any archaeological features present, and no other considerations regarding the trench positioning, a trenching strategy is likely to be designed to be parallel or perpendicular to the predominant alignment of the evaluation area. If nothing else this is a reflection of human nature, and the desire for order and 'neatness'.

A3.2.3 Assessment of the simulations

The effectiveness of the arrays was then assessed by turning on the archaeological layers, for each and then for all periods present on the site. The queries posed, and the scoring system used are described in Section 2.1.4. The results are shown in Tables A3.1-6.

A3.2.4 *Quantification of the success of simulations*

In order to provide an objective measure of the success of the various trenching simulations, a means of quantifying the results was sought. It was decided that the only way a computer could actually judge the success of a simulated trenching array was to calculate the actual area of archaeology lying within its boundaries. By also calculating the total area of all the archaeology revealed on the site, the quantity of archaeology detected by the trenching could be shown as a percentage of the total. For example, the exercise could examine whether on a variety of real sites, a trenching strategy of 5% revealed 5% of the archaeology present. Although the actual calculation of the areas is achieved easily by the computer, the process is by no means entirely automated. For each calculation the site plan must be carefully prepared for this type of analysis, and the process must be closely monitored in order to ensure that the computer is calculating the correct areas. Therefore, the whole process was relatively time consuming.

To calculate the total area of the archaeology on a site, a copy of the digital site plan was made in AutoCAD MAP 2000, and prepared so that information such as the site boundary was removed, and only the archaeological features were present. The polygons making up the drawing were then exploded, and cleaned up using various functions of the 'drawing cleanup' utility of MAP 2000. This process would have to be repeated a number of times, with slightly different parameters, until the drawing was 'clean' enough to attempt topology creation (a topology is an intelligent relationship between points or polygons, where information concerning the properties of the individual points or polygons is stored).

A polygon topology could then be created for the archaeology in the drawing, once again using MAP 2000 functions. This process requires a very high-quality drawing, and in most cases despite the previous clean-up process the topology creation would fail, and the drawing would have to be painstakingly scrutinised, and cleaned further 'by hand'. It would often take a number of such attempts before the topology could be successfully created. Having created a topology, the drawing would be 'intelligent' enough to, amongst other things, calculate the precise area of any of the drawing's polygons. However, the program could not distinguish between a polygon representing an archaeological feature, and a polygon representing an area of natural enclosed completely by archaeological features. Therefore the created topology was examined closely, and any such bogus polygons were 'deactivated' so that they would be excluded from subsequent queries.

At this stage a topology query was written and run to output a list of the calculated areas of all the individual polygons, each of which represented a single archaeological feature. It was then a simple matter to calculate the total area of archaeological features on the site.

In order to calculate the area of archaeology revealed by the trenching simulations, it was necessary to create a number of other topologies, one for each array tested. Each one of the trenching topologies then allowed an 'overlay topology' query to be run, in order to produce a drawing showing only the archaeological features present in the evaluation trenches. This result was then queried again to produce a list of the areas covered by archaeological features, and hence a percentage of the total archaeology could be deduced.

A3.2.5 *Assessment of the range of variation in a simulation*

In order to assess best- and worst-case trenching, arrays were positioned with archaeological layers open and were moved by the experimenter until the most and least effective position was reached. Of course, in these circumstances, the decision as to what is the best and worst outcome was subjective, but it was felt that this process was still a useful technique, for assessing the inherent variability in the possible outcomes of using a given evaluation strategy.

A second series of experiments were conducted to assess the range of results actually achieved, in a given number of applications of the same trenching array on the same site. From these results an average score for the technique could be reached, for comparison with the corresponding score achieved by the single 'random' simulation previously conducted. The first position of the array was produced by the 'random' method, as above, and then a further eleven positions were simulated in relation to it, giving a total of twelve. The location of the subsequent simulations was based on moving the original position 10 m further to the east with each successive simulation, and this was repeated six times, until the trenches were in the original position. The same process was then repeated six times by moving the array north 10 m, so that in total, simulations of the same trench array was carried out a dozen times, each one being in a slightly different position. A sequential sampling test suggests that the final results were stable.

Table A3.1 Quantification of the success of the simulations (random poisitions): All archaeology

Array Type	Sample fraction	Thurnham	Northumberland Bottom	White Horse Stone	Tutt Hill	Westhawk	Thanet Way	Ramsgate Harbour	Whitfield Eastry	Tesco Ramsgate	Elms Farm	Stansted	Yarnton Site 7
1. Standard grid (30m × 2m)	2%	4	7	6	5	13	8	8	4	9		10	4
	3%	8	6	8	5	11	9	8	7	10		12	9
	4%	7	11	12									
	5%	10	11	9	11	12	15	8	6	12		15	15
	10%	13	14	15	12	15	14	13	7	15		15	15
2. Grid with short trenches (20m × 2m)	2%	3	5	7									
	3%	7	7	11									
	4%	9	10	11									
	5%	10	11	13									
	10%	13	14	15									
3. Grid with wide trenches (30m × 4m)	2%	0	5	1									
	3%	4	4	3									
	4%	6	7	12									
	5%	4	7	13									
	10%	11	15	15									
4. Parallel array	2%	1	6	5	7	14	13	6	2	10		8	3
	3%	9	6	8	7	13	11	6	5	9		11	7
	4%	11	11	12									
	5%	10	12	11	13	15	10	10	9	11		15	4
	10%	14	15	14	12	15	13	12	12	13		15	11
5. Continuous trenching	2%	0	1	10									
	3%	2	2	4									
	4%	7	8	11									
	5%	11	7	10									
	10%	13	15	15				12					
6. Centre-line trenching		7	6	6									
7. 'Ramsgate Harbour' array		6	11	7									
8. Test pits		1	1	1									
Proposed trenching												13	

Out of possible 15 points

93

Table A3.2 Simulation results (random positions): Neolithic and Bronze Age

Array Type	Sample fraction	Thurnham	Northumberland Bottom	White Horse Stone	Tutt Hill	Westhawk	Thanet Way	Ramsgate Harbour	Whitfield Eastry	Tesco Ramsgate	Elms Farm	Stansted	Yarnton Site 7
1. Standard grid (30m x 2m)	2%	0	4	0	9	11	2	5	2	2	5	0	0
	3%	0	0	5	9	6	8	6	2	9		0	1
	4%	4	7	7									
	5%	4	5	0	9	10	10	5	2	11		11	10
	10%	8	9	12	11	12	12	8	9	12		11	12
2. Grid with short trenches (20m x 2m)	2%	0	3	0									
	3%	0	4	2									
	4%	0	4	9									
	5%	5	5	3									
	10%	8	9	12									
3. Grid with wide trenches (30m x 4m)	2%	0	0	0									
	3%	0	1	0									
	4%	1	4	9									
	5%	0	2	9									
	10%	3	9	12									
4. Parallel array	2%	0	1	2	8	3	9	1	2	10		0	3
	3%	4	0	0	7	6	10	2	2	6		0	7
	4%	9	5	12									
	5%	0	7	6	11	10	8	2	2	4		9	2
	10%	10	10	10	11	10	12	9	7	11		12	7
5. Continuous trenching	2%	0	2	5									
	3%	7	1	0									
	4%	4	8	4									
	5%	4	1	5									
	10%	8	12	12				8					
6. Centre-line trenching		4	1	4									
7. 'Ramsgate Harbour' array		0	1	8									
8. Test pits		0	0	1									
Proposed trenching												5	

Out of possible 12 points

Table A3.3 Simulation results (random positions): Iron Age

Array Type	Sample fraction	Thurnham	Northumberland Bottom	White Horse Stone	Tutt Hill	Westhawk	Thanet Way	Ramsgate Harbour	Whitfield Eastry	Tesco Ramsgate	Elms Farm	Stansted	Yarnton Site 7
1. Standard grid (30m x 2m)	2%	4	5	4	1		0	8	7			9	
	3%	4	5	10	1		0	9	6			11	
	4%	0	6	10	7		11	6	9			12	
	5%	4	7	9	8		0	10	11			12	
	10%	7	11	11									
2. Grid with short trenches (20m x 2m)	2%	1	3	1									
	3%	3	5	6									
	4%	7	6	8									
	5%	8	9	8									
	10%	7	11	11									
3. Grid with wide trenches (30m x 4m)	2%	6	0	3									
	3%	4	0	2									
	4%	2	7	6									
	5%	0	5	10									
	10%	6	9	12									
4. Parallel array	2%	0	4	2	4		0	7	4			8	
	3%	3	5	8	3		0	5	4			10	
	4%	4	9	9	9		0	7	7			11	
	5%	9	12	2	7		6	10	11			12	
	10%	10	12	11									
5. Continuous trenching	2%	0	0	2									
	3%	0	0	0									
	4%	6	6	1									
	5%	9	7	7									
	10%	8	12	8				8					
6. Centre-line trenching		4	6	0									
7. 'Ramsgate Harbour' array		5	7	1									
8. Test pits		0	1	0									
Proposed trenching												10	

Out of possible 12 points

Table A3.4 Simulation results (random positions): Roman

Array Type	Sample fraction	Thurnham	Northumberland Bottom	White Horse Stone	Tutt Hill	Westhawk	Thanet Way	Ramsgate Harbour	Whitfield Eastry	Tesco Ramsgate	Elms Farm	Stansted	Yarnton Site 7
1. Standard grid (30m x 2m)	2%	2	5	7		8	9					9	8
	3%	7	9	9		8	9					10	11
	4%	5	9	12									
	5%	8	11	8		10	12					12	12
	10%	12	10	11		12	12					12	12
2. Grid with short trenches (20m x 2m)	2%	3	4	9									
	3%	5	7	9									
	4%	8	7	12									
	5%	9	10	12									
	10%	12	10	11									
3. Grid with wide trenches (30m x 4m)	2%	0	4	1									
	3%	0	3	3									
	4%	5	4	11									
	5%	4	8	9									
	10%	8	12	12									
4. Parallel array	2%	2	7	2		9	10					5	0
	3%	9	3	9		11	9					9	0
	4%	12	7	10									
	5%	9	5	12		11	9					9	7
	10%	12	10	11		11	11					12	8
5. Continuous trenching	2%	0	1	7									
	3%	1	2	8									
	4%	5	3	8									
	5%	8	7	12									
	10%	9	12	12				8					
6. Centre-line trenching		1	6	7									
7. 'Ramsgate Harbour' array		5	8	8									
8. Test pits		2	2	2									
Proposed trenching												10	

Out of possible 12 points

Table A3.5 Simulation results (random positions): Early medieval/Anglo-Saxon

Array Type	Sample fraction	Thurnham	Northumberland Bottom	White Horse Stone	Tutt Hill	Westhawk	Thanet Way	Ramsgate Harbour	Whitfield Eastry	Tesco Ramsgate	Elms Farm	Stansted	Yarnton Site 7
1. Standard grid (30m x 2m)	2%						0	1	0	4			
	3%						0	1	4	7			
	4%												
	5%						12	1	0	10			
	10%						11	10	0	12			
2. Grid with short trenches (20m x 4m)	2%												
	3%												
	4%												
	5%												
	10%												
3. Grid with wide trenches (30m x 2m)	2%												
	3%												
	4%												
	5%												
	10%												
4. Parallel array	2%						10	0	0	0			
	3%						9	0	5	1			
	4%												
	5%						0	10	6	6			
	10%						0	0	4	10			
5. Continuous trenching	2%												
	3%												
	4%												
	5%												
	10%												
6. Centre-line trenching								1					
7. 'Ramsgate Harbour' array													
8. Test pits													
Proposed trenching													

Out of possible 12 points

Table A3.6 Simulation results (random positions): Medieval

Array Type	Sample fraction	Thurnham	Northumberland Bottom	White Horse Stone	Tutt Hill	Westhawk	Thanet Way	Ramsgate Harbour	Whitfield Eastry	Tesco Ramsgate	Elms Farm	Stansted	Yarnton Site 7
1. Standard grid (30m x 2m)	2%	6	9	6		11	12			5		11	0
	3%	8	8	12		12	1			10		12	11
	4%	9	8	10									
	5%	11	11	11		12	11			12		11	12
	10%	12	11	11		12	12			12		12	12
2. Grid with short trenches (20m x 2m)	2%	3	4	1									
	3%	9	7	6									
	4%	9	9	9									
	5%	10	10	12									
	10%	12	11	11									
3. Grid with wide trenches (30m x 4m)	2%	0	2	1									
	3%	6	2	0									
	4%	5	5	7									
	5%	2	8	11									
	10%	11	12	10									
4. Parallel array	2%	0	6	7		10	11			0		8	11
	3%	7	4	7		11	5			3		9	11
	4%	9	5	9									
	5%	12	10	6		9	9			10		12	11
	10%	9	12	12		11	10			9		12	11
5. Continuous trenching	2%	0	1	4									
	3%	0	7	10									
	4%	1	7	11									
	5%	10	9	9									
	10%	12	10	11									
6. Centre-line trenching		2	7	11									
7. 'Ramsgate Harbour' array		3	8	10									
8. Test pits		0	0	4									
Proposed trenching												8	

Out of possible 12 points

INDEX

Note: Figures are indicated by *italic* page numbers. There may also be textual references on these pages.

A aerial photography 2, 84, 86
aims and objectives 5
alluvium 2, 5, 14, 18, *20,* 27, 54, 63, 83
    and database queries 10
Anglo-Saxon period viii, 5, 9, 10, 15, 60, *61,* 62
    cemeteries 62
    desk-based assessment 21, 52
    evaluating remains 55
    fieldwalking 23, 53, 58
    geophysical survey 27, 31, 61, 83
    machine trenching 31
    settlement location 1
    simulated trench array 43, 50, 59, 63, 97
    see also early medieval period; sunken-featured buildings
archaeologist skill/experience 50
AutoCAD 2000 6, 10, 90
AutoCAD MAP 2000 6, 91

B Badsey 1 Association soil 81
Best Value 12-13
    see also cost-effectiveness
Boarley Farm, Kent *see* White Horse Stone
boreholes 2, 28-9
    site questionnaire 71
boundary ditches, medieval 27
brickearth geologies 33
Bronze Age vii, viii, 5, 9, 15, 59, *60,* 62
    late 9
        see also Iron Age
    desk-based assessment 21
    evaluating remains 55
    fieldwalking 23, 52, 61
    geophysical survey 27, 54, 58, 82
    machine trenching 31
    simulated trench array 9, 36, 37, 38, 43, *44,* 45, 47, 48, 50, 59, 94
    and site geology 18
buildings
    post-in-slot 86
    timber 86
    see also posthole structures; sunken-featured buildings; Thurnham Roman Villa
burials 62
    Iron Age 9
    Roman 9, 80
    early medieval/Anglo-Saxon 9

C Channel Tunnel Rail Link (CTRL) 3, 7, 23
    see also Northumberland Bottom; Thurnham Roman Villa, Kent; Tutt Hill, Kent; White Horse Stone
Church Road, Kent *see* Northumberland Bottom
colluvium 2, 5, 14, 18, *20,* 29, 54, 63, 81
    and database queries 10
computer simulations 10-12
    trench arrays 34-51, *34, 38-44, 46-7,* 59, 90-8
cost-effectiveness vii, 2, 12-13, 32, 52-7, *53,* 60, 61, 62
cropmarks, Northumberland Bottom 21

crops 21, 78, 80, 82, 84
CTRL *see* Channel Tunnel Rail Link

D   database 6
   querying 7-10
desk-based assessment vii, 6, 14, 58, 62
   cost-effectiveness 52
   and development size 16
   site questionnaire 68
   success of 21-3, *22*, 29, 31, 32
   digital data 2, 6-7, 63
errors in 79
   see also computer simulations

E   early medieval period vii, viii, 9, 15, *61*
   desk-based assessment 21
   geophysical survey 27
   machine trenching 31
   simulated trench array 43, *44*, 59, 97
   see also Anglo-Saxon period
Eastry/Whitfield Bypass *see* Whitfield to Eastry Bypass
Elms Farm, Essex *3*, 5, 16, 18, 63
   digital site plan 11
   evaluation techniques employed 15
   geophysical survey 20, 32, 54
   physical attributes 14
   simulated trench array 34, 93-8
   strip, map and sample 56
evaluation trenching *see* trench evaluation
excavation, site questionnaire 73

F   field boundaries 83
fieldwalking vii, 2, 14-15, 62
   cost-effectiveness 52-3
   development size 16
   recent land use 20
   site geology 18, 19
   site questionnaire 69
   success of 23, *24-5*, 26, 29, 31, 32, 33, 58, 59, 60, *61*
   weather and ground conditions 21
floodplain 2
form: evaluation techniques 7, *8*
Framework Archaeology, Stansted 23, 32
funerary monuments & enclosures 9, 27, 32, 54, 59, 62, 83
   and site geology 18

G   Geographic Information System (GIS) 6, 7, 79
geology 5, 14, 33, 63, 83
   database queries 10
   site location 1-2
   success of techniques 18, *19, 20*
geophysical survey vii, 10, 14-15, 23, 76-89
   cost-effectiveness 52, 53-4
   development size 16
   interpretation of data 88
   machine trenching *4*
   magnetometer survey *27, 60, 77, 78*, 80-3, 85-7, *85*
   recent land use 20
   resistivity survey 77, 78, 80, 81, 83-5, *85*
   site geology 1-2, 18, *19*
   site questionnaire 70

success of technique 26-8, *26, 29,* 31, 32, 33, 58, 59-60, 61
survey objectives 87-8
weather and ground conditions 21
see also individual sites
GIS (Geographic Information System) 6, 7, 79
Ground Penetrating Radar (GPR) 76, 77

H hut circles, Yarnton Cresswell Field 83

I identification of remains 33
Iron Age viii, 9, 15, *60,* 61, 62
   desk-based assessment 21
   and development size 16, *17*
   fieldwalking 23, 53
   geophysical survey 27, 83
   machine trenching 30, 59
   settlement location 1
   simulated trench array 36, 37, *44,* 47, 48, 50, 95
   and site geology 18, 19-20

K Kelmscot and Thames Association soils 83

L land use, and success of techniques 20, *21*
long enclosures 27, 54

M machine trenching 1, 15
   cost-effectiveness vii, 52, 54
   development size 16
   and geophysics *4*
   success of 23, 29-32, *30, 31,* 33, 58-9, 60
magnetometer survey *see* geophysical survey
Manston Road, Ramsgate (Tesco) *see* Tesco, Manston Road, Ramsgate
medieval period viii, 9, 60, *61,* 62-3
   desk-based assessment 21
   evaluating remains 55
   geophysical survey 27, 83
   machine trenching 30
   simulated trench array 36, 37, 38, 43, *44,* 47, 49, 59, 98
   strip, map and sample 57
   see also Anglo-Saxon period; early medieval period
metal detecting 23, 26, 60

N Neolithic period viii, 2, 5, 9, 15, 29, 59, *60,* 62
   desk-based assessment 21, 52
   evaluating remains 55
   fieldwalking 23, 52, 61
   geophysical survey 27, 54, 82, 83
   machine trenching 31
   posthole structure 11
   settlement location 1
   simulated trench array 36, 37, 38, 43, *44,* 45, 47, 48, 59, 94
   and site geology 18
   strip, map and sample 55
Northumberland Bottom *3,* 16
   desk-based assessment 21
   evaluation techniques employed 15
   machine trenching 54
   physical attributes 14
   simulated trench array 34, 36, 47, 48, 93-8

O Ordnance Survey 79
overburden, depth of 14, 63, 81
 database queries 10
 success of techniques 18, 19-20, *20*

P parallel trench arrays *see* trench arrays
Planning Policy Guidance Note 16 (PPG 16) 76
posthole structures 11, 28, 47, 54, 58, 60, 83, 86, 87
pottery *25*

Q questionnaire 6, 7, 12, 67-75

R Ramsgate, Kent *see* Tesco, Manston Road, Ramsgate
Ramsgate Harbour Approach Road, Kent *3, 5, 16*
 boreholes & test pits 28
 colluvial deposits 18
 evaluation techniques employed 15
 machine trenching 31, 54
 metal detecting 23
 physical attributes 14
 simulated trench array *34, 36, 38, 41*, 59, 93-8
 strip, map and sample 56
resistivity survey *see* geophysical survey
ridge-and-furrow cultivation 82, 83
ring ditches 27, 54, 58, 86
Roman period vii, viii, 60, *61*, 62-3, 80
 boreholes/test pits 29
 burials and ritual sites 9, 80
 desk-based assessment 21
 and development size 16, *17*
 evaluating remains 55
 fieldwalking 19, 23, 52, 60
 geophysical survey 27, 28, 54, 58, 60
 machine trenching 30
 metal detecting 23
 road 80
 simulated trench array 36, 37, 38, 43, *44*, 49, 50, 59, 96
 site geology 18, 19
 strip, map and sample 56
 villas 1, 56
 see also Thurnham Roman Villa
Romano-British period 50, 62
 strip, map and sample 57

S Saxon period *see* Anglo-Saxon period
scoring system 9-10
seminars 6
site database *see* database
site questionnaire *see* questionnaire
skill/experience of archaeologist 50
soil sieving 29
soil stripping 13
standard grid trench arrays *see* trench arrays
Stansted, Essex *3, 5, 16*
 cost-effectiveness 32
 evaluation techniques employed 15
 fieldwalking 23, *25,* 32, 52, 58
 physical attributes 14
 simulated trench array 93-8
 site geology 18
 strip, map and sample 32, 56

statistical procedures, geophysical survey 79-80
strip, map and sample viii, 13, 32
    cost-effectiveness 55-7, 62
sunken-featured buildings 27, 31, 60, 61

T   Tesco, Manston Road, Ramsgate *3*, 5, 16
    evaluation techniques employed 15, 60
    machine trenching 54
    physical attributes 14
    simulated trench array 45, 93-8
    strip, map and sample 56
test pits 28-9, 38, 39, 59
    cost-effectiveness 52, 54
    site questionnaire 71
Thames and Kelmscot Association soils 83
Thanet Way, Kent *3*, 5, 16
    desk-based assessment 21, 23, 52
    evaluation techniques employed 15
    geophysical survey 27, 32, 54, 78, 81, 86, *87*, 88
    physical attributes 14
    simulated trench array 93-8
    and site geology 18
    strip, map and sample 32, 56
Thurnham Roman Villa, Kent 3, 5, 16, *31*, 33
    desk-based assessment 21, 23
    evaluation techniques employed 15
    fieldwalking 23, *25*, 52
    machine trenching *31*
    magnetometer survey 78, 81, 83-4, 85-6, *85*, 88
    physical attributes 14
    resistivity survey 78, 81, 83, 84-5, *85*, 88
    simulated trench array 34, 36, *38*, 39, 45-7, 48, 93-8
    site geology 18
topography 78
trench arrays vii, 11-12, 63
    computer simulation 34-51, *34, 38-44, 46-7*, 59, 90-8
trench evaluation 21, 32, 62
    site questionnaire 72
trenching 61
    cost-effectiveness *55*
    machine *see* machine trenching
Tutt Hill, Kent *3*, 16
    boreholes & test pits 28
    evaluation techniques employed 15
    physical attributes 14
    simulated trench array 93-8

W   watching brief 7, 63
    site questionnaire 74
weather and ground conditions 21
Westhawk Farm, Ashford, Kent *3*, 5, 16, 87
    evaluation techniques employed 15
    geophysical survey *28, 29*, 32, 61, 78, 80-1, *82*, 88
    metal detecting 23
    physical attributes 14
    simulated trench array *46-7*, 93-8
    site geology 18
    weather and ground conditions 21
Westwell Leacon *see* Tutt Hill, Kent
Whickam 1 Association soils 80
White Horse Stone *3*, 5, 16, 33

boreholes & test pits 28, 29
colluvial deposits 18
desk-based assessment 52
evaluation techniques employed 15
geophysical survey 54
machine trenching 54
physical attributes 14
simulated trench array 34, 36, *39, 40,* 47-8, 93-8
strip, map and sample 55
Whitfield to Eastry Bypass *3, 5,* 16
evaluation techniques employed 15
fieldwalking 23
machine trenching 54
physical attributes 14
simulated trench array 93-8
strip, map and sample 56

Y Yarnton, Oxon 2, *3,* 5, 16
boreholes & test pits 28, 29
Cresswell Field, magnetometer survey 78, 81-3
evaluation techniques employed 15
fieldwalking 23, 32
geophysical survey 4, 21, 54, 59, 88
machine trenching *4,* 31-2, 54
magnetometer survey *27,* 60, 78, 81-3, *84*
physical attributes 14
Site 5, magnetometer survey *27,* 78, 81, 83, *84*
Site 7
geophysics and machine trenching *4*
simulated trench array 45, 93-8
and site geology 19
strip, map and sample 55, 56
Yarnton-Cassington Project 2